road toward the eastern giant

Erik J Churchill
Preface by Ricardo I. Rodriguez

Copyright © 2023 by Oscar Pulido

All rights reserved. No part of this publication may be reproduced, distributed, or transmitted in any form or by any means, including photocopying, recording, or other electronic or mechanical methods, without the prior written permission of the author, except in the case of brief quotations embodied in critical reviews and certain other noncommercial uses permitted by copyright law.

ISBN: 9798395197108

Scriptures used are taken from the New International Version, copyright © 1973, 1978, 1984 by International Bible Society.

Cover Design: Stephanie Pinilla

For More Information: erikjchurchill@gmail.com

Road Towards the Eastern Giant Revised Edition 2023

Revised by Margaret J Pulido and Erik J Churchill

To the Pulido family,
whose lives, unconditional love,
passion, and bravery, draw me closer
to Jesus

We are too young to realize that certain things are impossible... So we will do them anyway.

- William Pitt (the young)

Preface

And finally, there we were, standing on the top of that immense glacier; at the foot of the Amie Machen, the seven thousand-meter-high colossal peak crowned by an impressive and everlasting sheet of ice and snow. This was one of the many sites where Tibetan pilgrims went to offer sacrifice and carry out their pilgrimage. We were on the Roof of the World – more than eighteen thousand kilometres from our Colombian homeland.

We gathered our strength as much as we could and started to shout our lungs out over the land below and before us, declaring the scriptures, declaring that these were also the lands of our Lord, and that the Kingdom of God had come closer; that Christianity would flourish here too. That these uncultivated lands covered in darkness would now be illuminated by the truth and light of Christ. We also shouted and called out the Latin Americans, naming each nation; so that they would join the stream of God's river and take part in the building of the Kingdom... we shouted to the wind. We shouted without stopping as we looked to the sparkling-white heights... we called from the bottom of our hearts, and we knew we were being heard!

Victor was the one who took me on my first visit to China and Tibet. He personally and daily introduced me to the culture, the language, and the friends. Victor took me on the roads he knew, for he had walked them for many years. The unconditional love for China and Tibet, which he had cultivated for most of his life, became contagious to me. It was a love he was passionate about, even though it was a painful love.

Shut up or ya dead!

1

Suddenly, multiple gunshots broke the stillness of the tropical surroundings. They came from close by, from the line where the clearing met the dark, thick jungle. Immediately, desperate screams for help ensued. As he sprinted out of his living room onto the muddy porch, Victor saw his son - Oscar - running, slipping, and sliding down the steep dirt bank away from the gunshots towards the house. He was shouting at the top of his voice.

"Where are mum and Nats? Stay indoors and call the police. We're under attack!"

As he lifted his eyes beyond Oscar towards the hill west of the camp, Victor saw the five men who had emerged from the jungle. One was now threatening Kevin Prins, YWAM director for Trinidad and Tobago, while the others were trying to force open the vehicle where his wife and daughter, still in shock, were locked in from the inside. All the assailants were armed; some with handguns, one had a machete, and another was wielding a shotgun. They were all wearing carnival masks, both plain white and clown-looking in appearance. Victor ran the sixty to a hundred meters uphill to the site where the chaos came from. There he met Kevin, who was retreating slowly in an attempt to draw the masked men away from his family.

Mark, another missionary, had come to help from the north side of the Prins' house and couldn't see what was going on. He thought the screams were due to an encounter with a giant snake or an alligator. Once he emerged, he found himself staring down the barrel of the shotgun while the shooter demanded that he lie down.

"Give me all ya have!" he shouted at Mark, assuming every white foreigner shared a bank account with Elon Musk.

"I only have Jesus," responded the missionary.

"Give me all ya have or a' kill ya!" said the assailant even louder.

"I just told you. All I have is Jesus."

Upon hearing this, the mask could not hide the man's confusion as he retreated from Mark and joined the others. Meanwhile, Sue and Alyssa Prins were still inside the vehicle they had arrived in a few moments ago. The three men surrounding the car were desperately trying to break in. First, one of the men fired his gun at the door handle, and then another struck the door fiercely with his machete. After that, everything was a mix of shouting, screaming, and shots fired. Soon, blood patches on the dry, hot sand paved the road.

Others, such as Patrick and Oscar, had emerged once again. They started running up the hill with anything that came to hand, machetes or axes. Victor had arrived to help Kevin, who was now staggering downhill, clutching his throat. But before Victor could do anything, he turned to look at the vehicle. He found himself face to face with one of the masked men wearing a white mask, pointing a gun at his head no more than four meters away.

Something unexpected happened. Instead of retreating, kneeling, or even throwing his hands up, Victor shook with rage and shouted at his enemy:

"Get out of my territory right now, in Jesus' name!"

"Shut up or ya dead!" the assailant shouted back, taking half a step towards Victor, angry for being challenged by this unarmed foreigner.

"You leave this place right now. This is my property, and I am under God's authority!" shouted Victor in his best English.

"I swear I'm going to kill ya if ya say anotha word!"

These were the last words that came out of the masked man's mouth before everything stood still for Victor. It was a single confusing moment for all those close by. The only sure thing was that the assailant pulled the trigger.

In the Valley of the Shadow of Death

2

Let's go back many years to the city of Bogota in the 1960s, in the beautiful country of Colombia. As a young Latin American son of a catholic mother and a father who was absent for most of his life, Victor lived in search of the best things in life. All of us, at some point, reach a possible 'defining moment' when we ask the questions: Who am I? Where do I come from? And where am I going? Such questions were present in Victor's teenage years but without answers. Nevertheless, he somehow tried to find them in the sporting arena. He was quite a natural athlete in many sports but excelled in football. He also had a great passion for boxing, which led him to be the best fighter in the Antonio Galan neighborhood. He even set up his own garage boxing gymnasium. And like most of his young relatives and friends, he used these sports to express his search for identity, to which he could find no answer.

Mr. José - better known as Don Chepe - Victor's father - spent time in the infantry and then studied architecture. He founded a construction company. He built many schools and universities, some well-known in the Department of Cundinamarca. Doña Blanca took care of the seven children single-handedly – not that there was any choice for her since Don Chepe had his 'main' family with another woman on the other side of Bogota. Most of the time, he was involved in some construction project out of town. When he visited Victor and the rest of the family (three daughters, four sons, and Doña Blanca, Victor's mother), he always brought gifts with him. This was his way of showing love to his family. Despite the gifts and presents, there was never an atmosphere of joy or laughter leading up to or during his visits. When the family heard news that Don Chepe would visit them, in spite of the anticipation of receiving the gifts and clothes he would bring with him, the mood in the house would become highly sober. If a negative school report happened to show up, or a complaint about the children from one of the neighbors was heard, there was a certainty of receiving a sure and firm telling-off; for the boys, it was usually in the form of a beating. None of the young rascals would be able to breathe with tranquillity when their father was around, all too aware of his unpredictable nature.

It wasn't that Don Chepe wanted to be feared, cruel, or remembered for his beatings, but he could only share with his family what he, in turn, had received from his own father. He employed the same method of sharing his affections with his children as he learned from his father: through gifts, money, and an icy and military manner, as the macho culture is famous for. When asked, not once could Victor remember his father saying the words "I love you" to him or any of his siblings or smiling at him. These behaviors tend to pass through families from one generation to the other, and only some manage to break the cycle. So, my dear reader, I invite you to identify the behaviors exhibited in your family and yourself that may have been passed on by earlier generations. If any of them fall short of being 'acts of blessing,' God can help remove them from your life if you ask Him.

In 1970, a few weeks after the football world cup ended, Don Chepe's life also ended; he died of a heart attack. Despite the loss, the brothers and sisters inhaled a fresh breath of freedom into their daily life. Not a moral freedom but a freedom to do whatever lured their appetites, especially since they each received a part of the inheritance. Before long, addictions came knocking at the door. When they came knocking at Victor's door, he was coaching a football team. There were high expectations for the team since Victor was very disciplined and committed to whatever he set his mind to do, a good trait learned from his father. There was a great sense of brotherhood amongst the team, which caused them all to go together in pursuit of the 'lost sheep' of the group. They noted one of their friends had stopped coming to the practices. They soon heard this was due to constantly being busy smoking marihuana. Shortly after, they crashed one of the parties he was at to rescue him from this vice – which didn't turn out well at all. Instead of saving him from this habit, they all got a taste of it and ended up hooked. Victor noted the darkness in his life increasing with every puff as time passed. He was falling, and he knew it. So he tried to free himself, but with every failure, his despair grew; In the words of Jesus himself:

"Apart from me, you can do nothing."

Victor knew little about Jesus, God, or the Bible.

Each day the chains of drugs and alcohol tightened around his neck. As anyone without fear of God, Victor and his brothers had no respect for man or woman, they sought to establish themselves with power and strength as the most daring youth in the area. With the increase in drugs, drunkenness, and parties, their love and commitment to football decreased to null; on the other hand, street fights and brawls became everyday events. A friend of a friend invited Victor and his friends one day to a party. There would be dancing with pretty girls and a lot of beer. After the evening, people started to leave with strange smiles on their faces as drunks have. At that moment, one of the other lads walked past Victor and his group with two girls, one in each arm. On seeing him, Federico - Victor's younger brother - shouted at the passerby:

"Lend me one of those beauties, will ya?" referring to the guy's lady-friends, to which he replied, losing his smile:

"Sure, just give me a second. I'll be right back." But, unfortunately, the ironic tone in his voice was too subtle for drunk Federico to pick up.

Federico, Victor, and the rest of the group hadn't realized that this young man they had just insulted was the chief of a neighboring enemy street gang. And since everyone on Victor's side who was watching walked away assuming that Federico's joke had been taken lightly - what a surprise they were in for. As they walked away from the party, maybe fifteen minutes later, they were approached by a larger crew of about twenty gangsters, armed to their teeth with clubs, belts with sharpened buckles, iron chains, and awful language. Their leader, the young man who had assured Federico he would bring him one of his girls, stepped forward.

"So, who was the idiot who asked me for one of my ladies?"

For some reason, the leader didn't recognize Federico immediately, thanks to the alcohol. This allowed Federico to sneak up on him and say:

"It was me!" While landing a hefty blow on the leader's nose, with such a shock that it knocked him to the ground.

Seeing their leader on the ground, with substantial blood pouring from his nose, they got ready to attack. But Victor and his friends saw the chance to escape, and they would've taken it if wouldn't have been because Federico decided to challenge another member of the group. Federico - who obviously was under the effect of the many drinks he'd had - squared up to the rest of the gang and decided it was the right time to summon his best martial artist impressions; indeed, in his own mind, he was the spitting image of Jackie Chan. As he clumsily let his fists punch the air wildly in violent motions, which were accompanied by short Bruce Lee-style shouts as seen on television, one of the gangsters laughed mockingly and said,

"This drunk is all show and no fight. I'll give him a lesson!"

The gangster closed on him swiftly, only to be met by a substantial and sudden palm strike to the nose. Being drunk and earnestly believing himself to be Bruce Lee's mentor seemed to work for Federico; he broke his opponent's nose in one lucky strike. The rest of the gang was taken aback for some seconds and hesitated to move in on Victor's younger brother.

This allowed the rest of Victor's gang to regroup and begin their retreat. As they moved away, they defended each other with belts, sticks, clubs, or whatever they could find on their way, which turned out to be no easy feat. Victor's group was not only under fire from the other gang's pursuit, but as they went through the neighborhood, the mothers and aunts of the gangsters came out of their houses throwing stones, rotten food, or even wielding knives in a warning for them to leave the place as quickly as they could. They thought Victor's group was the instigator of the situation.

In these recurring violent encounters, some escaped, and some died. There wasn't much security on the Colombian streets at that time. This was a culture of gangs and hippies. In conversations about these earlier times, Victor remembered one or more of his friends who met their death with a bullet through the head.

For this reason, pursuing peace, the peace that Jesus offers, is always best. He said, "Peace I leave with you, my peace I give to you." We must walk in the Lord's peace. The Lord allowed Victor to walk away alive from many violent encounters throughout his early life. He had an excellent plan for his life, which would be fulfilled in the coming years.

Rescue

3

At the age of nineteen, two significant events were going on, simultaneously influencing Victor's life and driving him to extreme decisions. One was the hippie movement. At that time, one of the greatest icons of this movement - Jimmy Hendrix - took his own life by overdosing on narcotic substances. Jimmy and other significant figures in the hippie movement displayed suicide as a way to escape the 'meaninglessness of life' and the desperation in which they found themselves, unable to answer the fundamental questions of life's meaning and purpose.

Victor and his brothers were faithful followers of the hippie movement. They grew their hair long, and their clothes were the typical hippie colors of the 60s. And to cap things off, the use of drugs was a trademark that was proudly displayed to show their sense of belonging to the movement. The other event taking place in Victor's heart and mind was the desperate inner search for meaning for which he had found no answer. The desperation grew with every night. It seemed as if the pit of drugs and alcohol in which Victor looked for answers closed in around him and got ever deeper; until the sunlight could barely be seen at the top of the pit. Because of this, his passion for football was robbed too. The first event - Jimmy Hendrix's suicide - fueled with the amounting inner frustration provided what seemed to be a simple and swift escape from the desperation he was feeling. He made his decision.

One Saturday morning, Victor woke up more somber than ever before. He packed a few supplies into a small rucksack and left for his one-way journey to a farm in Fusagasuga, intent on taking his own life. Thoughts of his mother, brothers, and sisters clouded his mind, but he was decided. Voices whispered in his ears, 'When this is all over, there'll be no more pain, confusion, or this miserable existence.' They beckoned him to hurry to the goal he had in mind, convincing him that he was doing what was best for him. Victor could not recognize that each and every one of those thoughts was an assault from the enemy of his soul against his weak emotional and mental defenses. These voices and some precious memories of his family coursed through his mind as he rode the bus that would take him to his final destination. He arrived at the specified place in the countryside by early afternoon. He immediately proceeded to buy a combination of mushrooms and narcotics, which would be enough for him to carry out his secret plan.

Since he was walking in his last hours, Victor didn't fancy spending them alone, so he invited his three best friends along; his younger brother Federico and two others. As they approached one of the rich green hills next to a calm river in the vast and open land, the beauty of the environment had no influence on Victor's determination. They were all very communist in their way of thinking. As they sat beneath a tree on the hill, they asked him:

"What topic do you wish to be the last you ever talk about?"

The question must have come from everyone knowing Victor was a publicly confessed atheist. Victor answered their question.

"All right then, let's talk about the supposed existence
of God."

"As you wish," answered Federico, "Let's talk about God's existence. But as a brother and friend, I'll tell you face to face that God exists, whether you like it or not!"

What happened next could be compared to the sudden manifesting of a hurricane that threw all four of them on the ground. It's as if God honored the words of Victor's brother, "God exists, whether you like it or not." Victor couldn't describe what was happening; they didn't have denominational jargon to call it the Presence of God. But he knew that God himself was there, or at least close by. The fierce wind was beating the trees, creating the sound of creaking wood. Suddenly Victor's spiritual eyes were opened, and he got a terrifying and scary shock.

They were all on their knees, all but Victor. Unable to stand in God's presence, he lay flat on the ground. Only Victor experienced the events that followed in their totality. He slowly dawned into the consciousness that he was rising off the ground towards the sky. He soon realized he was doing so spiritually and consciously. Looking down, he saw his body lying face down on the grass - motionless. He could see his body, the untidy bundle of hair on his head attached to a skinny, abused, and neglected body. He looked destroyed. Tears came to his eyes caused by the sadness and grief caused by seeing his own body. He felt guilty for so badly treating the gift that God himself had given him. At that moment, he understood one thing: God gives us all a body to be a tool of blessing, minister to others, and take care of it as a house is taken care of, inside and out. Coming to that realization, Victor was overcome with a sudden chill of despair and fear, knowing that he hadn't fulfilled his responsibility and duty on earth and that, for some reason, he would be knocking on the gates of hell very shortly.

We all have spiritual ears and eyes just as we have physical ones. God opened Victors'. Immediately his attention was fixed on the tree, which he had just been sitting under, unable to look away. He could see the hundreds of leaves that adorned the trunk - they had facial expressions! They clapped their sides as excited and euphoric as a five-year-old waking up and realizing it was Christmas day. And just when he thought it couldn't get any better, all of a sudden, in unison and perfect harmony, they started to sing - the leaves began to sing!

"The Holy One is here! The Holy One is here. Holy! Holy! Holy!"

For a moment, Victor thought he and the whole world were going crazy. But he could feel a presence... the presence of God, enveloping him, and a soft voice said:

"Victor, do you want to die today?"

"Yes," he answered with shame and fear, "I'm tired of this world, I'm frustrated with life."

Victor was conscious of two things as he answered. Firstly, he was a sinner and had been sinning for most of his life. Secondly, he knew that the God who was present right there and then was utterly and entirely holy. Victor could see his own hands in the spiritual world. There were dirty, as was the rest of his body. But God cut his self-contemplation short and whisked him away, faster than any rocket, to some unexplored corner of the universe. Was it physical? Was it spiritual? He didn't know.

He instantly realized where he arrived wasn't hospitable, homely, or welcoming. It was a dark, cold, and terrible place. Fear was in the air; it was so thick that it could find its way deep under the skin and into the bones. He looked around and saw before him what resembled a gigantic cave. It had great width and height and was filled with a darkness that could almost be touched. But it wasn't the cave itself that filled Victor's heart with terror. Instead, he saw before him, inside the cave, a massive crowd of people dressed in grey robes. There were millions of them, and they filled the dark cavern. It was an immense waiting hall, a waiting room for hell. Everyone standing there was so horrified that their eyes were bloodshot. It's as if they knew what awaited them, and they were so overwhelmed with fear that they shook uncontrollably. Sounds filled the cave; sounds of wailing, of chattering teeth, and screaming. It was a nightmare. As the Bible says: 'and there shall be the weeping and the gnashing of teeth.'

Victor could do nothing but look at this terrible scene. Finally, he found a way to break his silence. He asked God desperately:

"Who are all those people? Why do they have so much fear? What will happen to them?"

"Victor," The Lord answered, "all those thousands before you committed suicide in their life on earth. I gave them life and Grace; I formed them in their mother's womb;

they were supposed to be temples of my Holy Spirit, but they destroyed it. They tremble because they know the doom they have chosen and what awaits them. You don't know yet, but they have seen it, and their time shall come; darkness awaits them."

After a moment, The Lord, with a voice full of compassion and tenderness, asked Victor,

"So, are you sure you want to die today?" It wasn't a question that required a Ph.D. or much deep meditation on Victor's part to be answered. He answered as desperate as a damned soul,

"No! Please! I don't want to die – please forgive me! I don't want to come to this horrible place."

Victor," again said The Lord, full of love for him, "I love you. Leave the drugs behind, along with the drunkenness; read the Bible and repent."

The young man didn't know much about the Bible; he knew his mother had one, but he'd never read it. He couldn't think of any of his friends who might have one. Victor was returned to his body at great speed as carried by the wind. He could feel God's love and the forgiveness carried out just moments ago. All the sins he had committed in the past had been erased, and a new story had begun. God's words resounded in his entire being: "I love you. Stop the drugs, and repent." As Victor's spirit again took up residence in his body, he stood up, took the remaining drugs in his pockets, and threw them into the river. He promised himself and God that he would never again consume such things. God's power and presence were over Victor in such a powerful way that he started to preach to his three companions. It wasn't a difficult task since they had been crying uncontrollably while Victor had his supernatural experience. They hadn't seen anything but had felt the powerful presence of God all around them.

The four friends left the farm, and as they headed for the road, they wept. The day had turned to night, around nine o'clock. They put much effort into leaving that 'place of sin' as fast as they could, thinking and fearing that maybe God would change His mind. And even though they were wrong in their theology, their hurry was to get as far away from that place before God's love would 'run out.' The whole experience had a profound impact on Victor and his friends and brother, who still wept as they stepped into the first bus that passed by. With an expression of shock and worry, the driver asked them if someone had just died or been murdered. The rest of the passengers just looked on. No one answered the driver, so Victor became the spokesman. He stood at the front of the bus, just behind the driver, and described to everyone the experience all four had just witnessed.

"If you don't repent, you will end up going to that horrifying place!" he said. The passengers grew pale, for they could see that he spoke with an authority not from himself but from God.

Upon arriving home, everything seemed as if nothing had happened, as if Victor's mother and siblings had been in an entirely different universe to that which had hosted the events that afternoon. The whole family was sitting around the television, watching a black and white transmission of a boxing match between the renowned Colombian Panbelle and some challenger. Finally, Victor walked into the living room with a resolution that would not be ignored. As he switched the TV off, he told his family about what had happened to him and his companions.

"Are you really enjoy watching these guys punching each other? Instead, repent!" he exclaimed after the story.

None of his brothers, not even his mother, had ever heard him speak in this fashion before; one by one, they started weeping. The presence and mercy of God were present at that moment, and none of them were confessing Christians. Yet some of them thought Victor could be pretty tired, the reason for such strange behavior.

"Lie down and sleep for a while; tomorrow will be a new day, and you'll feel different."

The next day, he woke up and felt exactly the same. That day he decided to have a walk in his local park, to try and speak with God again. Although he couldn't see anyone, and His presence wasn't as evident to the senses as it had been the day before, he expressed to God what he had felt and heard. He reminded Him that he didn't want to go to hell and didn't wish to return to a life of drugs. He added that he felt a bit lost since he had no one to guide him or teach him how to walk in this new story of His.

"I need someone to teach me! Please help me with that", he said.

The Lord then gave him a vision. He saw before him a typically dressed evangelical man with a black bible. Until then, Victor only knew that evangelicals were righteous and spiritual people; they weren't given to drugs and could most likely help him. He had seen these people walking to meetings and churches on Sundays in the past, but he now saw them in a new way. He used to make fun of them, but now he admired them and wanted to ask his mother whether or not she had any evangelical friends. The answer was no. So he resorted to the Google of his time: the phonebook.

There he found a total of six evangelical churches in the whole city of Bogota. As one of them answered the line, he asked for a "father" or "priest." Finally, they put him through to a local pastor. After talking for some time, the pastor visited him, and Victor told him about his experience with The Lord. The pastor led him to an understanding of the sacrifice of Jesus Christ and to repeat the famous confession of faith. Victor always said that this moment marked a tremendous turnaround in his life. Since then, he started attending church with the pastor as he took his first steps in a long life, holding God's hand. Little did Victor know that in two months, he would have an experience that would set him in a specific direction for the following many years of his life.

Victor's Mother Doña Blanca

The Debt

4

The Bible says in Romans 1:14, "I am debtor both to Greeks and to Barbarians, both to the wise and to the foolish." The Bible shows through Paul that we all have a debt to pay. We only rest once we pay it off. We have an obligation with South Americans, North Americans, Asians, Europeans, and Africans. This debt is the Gospel, the message of Jesus Christ that has been shared with us; it is our job to share it with the millions who have no idea who Jesus is.

Two months after dramatically encountering The Lord, Victor met a businessman in Bogota who offered him a job opportunity. Victor was on fire for Jesus and didn't waste this opportunity to share the Gospel with his new boss. The man was evidently interested in the Gospel. So much so that he asked Victor to come to his home three days in a row to explain more about the scriptures and how to live with Jesus. His interest was so great that he gave Victor money exclusively to buy him a Bible. Then they would be able to go to church together. The young evangelist was very about this. He was convinced that that same night this man would come to know Jesus in a personal way.

Upon arriving at the church service, the topic that night happened to be the devil - whose demons apparently weren't absent from the sermon either. A large part of the talk was focused on the "great" power and purpose of the enemy to attack anyone who decided to go against his evil schemes. Victor's boss, who was having his first "evangelical church" experience, became paler and paler as the minutes passed. Finally, at the end of the meeting, looking at Victor with fear, he said:

"Victor, I don't think it's a good idea for me to give the devil any reason to get mad at me. What the pastor said is true, and I can't be a part of it. I admire you, Victor, but I won't live a life fighting against such a devil. So take my Bible, and keep the change."

He left that place, shaking inside and out.

Victor couldn't understand what had happened. He had invited a non-Christian to church - a very willing non-Christian, ready to give his life to Jesus. But a devil-based sermon had scared him off. Who knew whether this man would have the same chance to get to know Jesus' love in the future? Needless to say, Victor left the building with his head dropped low, in a deep sense of frustration. At eleven at night, the darkness seemed thicker than ever as he walked home. Many doubts went around the mind and heart of the recently born-again follower of Jesus. In his own words, Victor felt dumbfounded and frustrated. Tears of sadness and anger rolled down his cheeks. In his grief, he looked to the dark sky and said,

"You didn't help me! That guy is going to go to hell and YOU didn't help me!"

As he neared his home, he continued to be angry and disappointed. His walk took him through an old park where he used to play football and sit down for chats with his friends for many years. As late and dark as the hour was, the swings and iron bars used as a public gym were still quite visible. At these hours, it stopped being an innocent recreational park and turned into a meeting point for drug consumers and addicts who tried to escape the imprisonment of daily routine; it was a hippie-designated area, and Victor used to be one of them. As he walked by, he saw a group of long-haired old friends sitting and talking on the grass. This didn't surprise him; he knew they were probably ingesting some sort of substance. What surprised him was what one of the guys said after running up to him suddenly.

"Victor! Brother, please come." "What's wrong?" Victor asked.

"We all heard that now...." he paused, "now you are a Christian... or evangelical or something, and it just happens that we had an experience with your God yesterday - and we want to be at peace with Him."

Victor walked with the skinny fellow back to the rest of the group. He saw that amongst them, there was a guest gnostic. He had been invited to try and explain Jesus because, quite obviously, they wanted to change. They wanted to quit their drugs. They described what had happened to them the day before. As they had been sitting in the same park - drinking and smoking - a Christian man walked towards them. He was handing out evangelical tracts and gave them some as he passed by. In their drunken and high state, one of them saw an opportunity for amusement. He took a tract in his hands, stood up, and started reading. Halfway through the reading, the "designated reader' began to cry, and as he continued reading, he wept louder and louder. The others were speechless, hanging onto every word as he kept reading. In the end, they were all crying. Finally, they decided they had to repent before God. All this happened through a tract without any human help.

They had already gotten rid of any drugs and alcohol they had in their possession. Still, they didn't have anyone to explain the message of salvation to them. They asked Victor then to break down the message of the Gospel for them and then to guide them in whatever steps were necessary to surrender their lives to Christ, for they knew that he was an evangelical. Apparently, the gnostic had been speaking to them for about two hours about the "mysteries" and philosophy of reincarnation. It didn't make any sense to them, and he knew it. The gnostic invited Victor to take the main seat among them. Victor sat down and described the dramatic events he had experienced about two months before. He followed up with the question Nicodemus presented to Jesus: What must I do to have eternal life? And Jesus answered: "Unless you become born again, you will not enter the kingdom of heaven." They talked about this subject in the middle of that old park at midnight. Finally, when he asked them,

"Who of you want to kneel with me and receive Jesus?" nine of them raised their hands and, full of joy, decided to give their lives to The Lord. Victor prayed for them one last time, placing his hands upon their heads, and left for home; with a massive smile. Even though he lost someone because of a terrifying sermon, he had been given nine in a simple park in less than an hour. Victor lay in his bed with a broad smile of delight and gratitude to God, but he didn't even suspect what would happen the next day.

In the early hours of the morning, at Doña Blanca's residence, knocks were heard on the front door. On opening, Victor found himself facing the nine from the night before.

"We've rented out a small garage. Could you be our pastor and hold church services there?" they exclaimed with full smiles.

"Wow, these guys are flying!" Victor thought. After agreeing to this, he encouraged them and sent them to invite others to the meeting. He also sent them to find Bibles, tracts, and teachings. The guys left and, amazingly, soon discovered a small quaint Christian bookstore in the city center (in those times, Christian bookstores in Colombia were a rare occurrence). To Victor and Federico's surprise, they arrived, each with their brand new Bible under their arm. These hippies were delighted with their Bibles, new books, guitars, and of course, dark shades that didn't come off even under cover of the garage. Then and there, the first-ever service began in the first church in the San Rafael neighborhood in Bogota. It started at seven in the evening, with many hippies sitting on the concrete floor of a random garage.

Victor had testified a lot in public but still felt some fear when faced with the prospect of giving a complete sermon in front of a multitude of people. So Federico was automatically assigned as the preacher for this first service. At the end of the message, many gave their lives to Jesus, including many men and women who had to stand and listen from the outside of the garage due to lack of space. Victor was left speechless by his younger brother's preaching skills. So much that he had to ask,

"What is your secret, brother? When did you learn to be such a public speaker? And when did you write such a message?"

"Well," replied Federico with a smile as he handed some tracts to Victor, "I'll tell you the secret. I buy these tracts written by this American guy - I think he's called Billy Graham. And I memorize his teachings; that's it!"

At that moment, something happened, just like when Esau gave up his birthright to Jacob. The anointing of preaching passed onto Victor. It was a flame that would turn into a forest fire.

As always, moments and events would put the young evangelist's faith to the test. On one occasion, walking at midnight, Victor saw an old friend of his. This friend had heard about Victor's new life as a follower of Jesus, so he asked him to pray since he had been consuming drugs a lot. Right there, in the middle of the street where they met, he knelt so that Victor would pray for him - which he did. Only God knows if the friend had repented truly in his heart, for on the third day, while trying to steal a bicycle, its owner drew his gun and shot the friend three times in the head. Where that lad is right now, Victor doesn't know; only God does. But this is the reality for many who have the opportunity to hear and receive the Gospel. As far as Victor is aware, two of those who were at that first service in San Rafael are pastors now; some have their own businesses, and many others are still passionate followers of Jesus.

One afternoon, two members of the anti-drug division of the police approached Victor; they asked to talk with him alone.

"We have heard reports that in your garage, many junkies and prostitutes are meeting up to possibly sell and consume drugs. Now we see that it's not the case. We want to congratulate you, pastor, for what you do with all these people. Keep it up!"

This wasn't the last time that this happened. Victor was visited many a time by different governmental divisions to inspect his meetings and services. Once they had seen what was going on, they gave glory to God, for they could see that many of the youngsters were quitting their drugs and living a better life, serving Jesus.

At the end of one of the services, once Victor had taken the initiative to preach, he invited all who wanted to receive forgiveness from Jesus to the front of the garage. Many raised their hands, but a voice came from the outside of the garage,

"Wait a moment; I have a question. Is that invitation for those of us on the outside too?"

"Of course! Come on in!" Replied Victor.

All those who wanted to receive Jesus in their hearts were ushered forward. There were many former drug dealers, and among them, three prostitutes. Seeing them, Victor had doubts in his heart concerning the sincerity of their conversion, but those doubts soon dissolved away. None of the three girls was absent in all the following services. On one occasion, the Holy Spirit descended upon the congregation, and one of the women, amid her own tears, confessed openly that she was selling drugs and was involved in prostitution. A year and a half later, she married one of Victor's friends, a pastor, and began to serve in that congregation. Until today they have been strong Christians, and they have two beautiful daughters.

Victor never forgot those two extraordinary nights and many others where the hand of God's mercy saved the lives of those addicts and prostitutes. It was by the grace of Jesus. For that reason, my dear reader, to you who know Jesus, Paul says: "I am debtor both to Greeks and to Barbarians, both to the wise and to the foolish." We are debtors to South Americans and non-South Americans and to Colombians and non-Colombians. Open your mouth, and God will fill it so you will bless those who don't know Jesus. For Victor, those nights of revival were just the beginning.

Pray for me, I'm in Agony

5

It had been some time since the San Rafael church was founded, and Victor's passion had not diminished one bit. On the contrary, it had grown like a small creek when joining the mighty Nile. It grew as he entered into deeper intimacy with the Holy Spirit. Victor was in the state you might call the "First Love" of a Christian. The Bible warns us to take care and not step out of our first love. During this time, an association of churches invited him to work with them by preaching in towns, cities, and municipalities. All this was to be done door to door, at a very personal level.

The project was to last more than a year. The schedule was filled; with little time for rest, but that didn't matter to Victor. He was filled with passion and fire for God. He would finish a weekend evangelism event on a Sunday night and start at a new church on a Monday with a different congregation. It was a time of great harvest. For the first time in his life, he worked as a volunteer without any salary and took up the challenge. He launched himself with God to live a life of faith and saw for himself how God supernaturally supplied his every need. Victor started to understand what it really meant to "live by faith." Just like the disciples and apostles in the primitive church, he was asked to leave everything behind and be ready to go even to death by walking with God and fulfilling the last commandment of Jesus. For Victor, surrendering all was like taking off the parachute, which he trusted to save him, should he fall, believing that God was the only one who could save him.

Victor's parachute was the fact that he was an excellent businessman and salesman. From a young age, he had worked that way. To let go of this, and dedicate his life to preaching the message of Jesus Christ, without a sure paycheque, was indeed the most visible way to take off his parachute. Victor started to see that his Lord would not let him fall. He provided everything for him, enough to travel by car, horse, bus, ship, and plane. All this provision came so that he would fulfill his part in the Great Task he was given as Jesus said just before ascending into heaven; "therefore, go, and make disciples of the nations, baptizing them in the name of the Father, and of the Son, and of the Holy Spirit; teaching them to keep all the commandments I have given you." The Lord Jesus left us all the job of taking the gospel to every creature and place on earth.

Victor had been invited to speak and edify the church in a region called Segovia, in the province of Antioquia. On the first night of the campaign, the Holy Spirit powerfully fell on the congregation, including on Victor. Amidst all this, he noticed the degenerated state of the old church building. The doors had cracks, and the hinges were rusty, like everything else made of metal in the church. Most of the windows were broken, and the constant dripping during the night testified to the roof's condition. At the end of the service that night, Victor stood back up behind the pulpit, and addressing the congregation he said:

"At night, we shall have our campaigns; but as long as there is daylight, we will fix this temple - because it's terrible!"

Everyone accepted the challenge joyfully and enthusiastically. The following day they all met outside the church building. Each had brought as many building materials as possible; each contributed strength, encouragement, and eagerness to restore the old house of prayer. This scene made Victor imagine how the early church might have been, all working together, giving from the generosity birthed in their hearts due to their love. Some gave brushes, others gave paint and other materials such as those needed to fix the leaky roof. Everyone shared the same spirit. As the work went on, the sound of hymns rose. And then it seemed as though the enemy decided to strike.

Victor had taken personal responsibility to fix the leaky roof; since he already had some experience doing this from his earlier years. He had already placed a ladder against the rooftop and started to climb it, but as soon as he reached the top, his footing suddenly slipped. For a long moment, Victor observed the world swirling all around him, with a concrete floor coming towards him faster and faster as he fell headfirst towards the concrete floor, landing with a loud crack. To Victor, it felt like the whole world had exploded, starting with his skull. Everything was gradually becoming darker before his eyes. He couldn't speak, he couldn't breathe, he couldn't do anything other than remain entirely still. He could vaguely see his Christian brothers and sisters run towards him, shouting desperately for help. He could hear them say things such as: "Our brother is dead!". Victor couldn't say a word, he thought he was already dead, or on the brink of becoming so, at least. In his agony, Victor prayed in his mind:

"My God! Help me to at least say goodbye to them," and gathering all his strength, he managed to let go a tiny whisper:

"Pray for me. I'm in agony."

As soon as they heard him speak, many of the men picked him up carefully, carried him to the pastor's room, and lay him on the bed. At this point, everything was almost pitch black from Victor's view.

Two old folks were in the room; they had to be at least 80 years old. They had seen Victor fall. They wore traditional Antioqueño outfits as tears ran down their wrinkly faces. Then, finally, they decided to make one last attempt to help Victor. They lay their hands on him as they lifted their heads to pray. As soon as their hands touched him, Victor saw a powerful shining light that broke through the darkness and went straight into his body, filling every atom of his being. Its potency was so strong that it caused him to sit straight up in bed as if the mattress had rejected him suddenly. The two elders were wide-eyed and speechless. Their tears of grief turned to tears of overwhelming joy. The news immediately spread through the town:

"The evangelist fell from the second floor headfirst and
he looks as if nothing ever happened!"

God had already given Victor a warning about this event occurring. Before he came to Segovia, he had been in Medellin; and there he had a dream. In this dream, he saw himself lying in a very particular box; a coffin. As he caught sight of his own face, he almost leaped out of bed. He wondered whether he would die soon; he believed the dream was some kind of sign from God, so he started a day and a half of fasting so that any evil plans in the spiritual world against him would be dismantled. Remembering this dream convinced him that God's grace was the only reason he wasn't dead at that moment.

When we work with The Lord, depending on Him, he might show us small sightings of events that have not yet come to pass to us or others as a warning to prepare and do spiritual warfare. If you are connected in relationship with The Lord, he could send you warning messages so that you pray, fast, and maybe prevent some small or great catastrophe.

The Man in the Coffee Field

6

One only sometimes knows the transcendence of what one does, and few have the privilege of seeing the fruit of the work the Lord has called them to do. Our greatest reward is in heaven; Jesus himself will be the one to give it to us.

Some years after his accident while fixing the church building in Segovia, Victor had an exciting encounter that reminded him of his own spiritual state of depression and desperation before having his encounter with the Lord. Victor was campaigning in another zone of Segovia, a beautiful place with high mountains covered in rich coffee plantations. After concluding some conferences with a church, he began a long walk to the next town since he had no horse provided on this occasion. The trail took him through some lush and bountiful coffee fields, with intense green leaves everywhere, sparkling as the sunlight hit the dew (think bollywood). There was also a river flowing at the bottom of the fields. He saw a young man in the distance as he walked on the riverbanks. As Victor drew closer, he judged that the stranger must have been about twenty years old. He was sitting alone - tears flowing down his face.

"Why are you crying?" Victor asked.

At first, the young man was naturally suspicious and defensive in the face of such a direct question. But he noted the passer-by's genuine concern and soon explained the reasons for his moist eyes. It turned out that this young man's girlfriend had ended their relationship. His grief was so deep that he considered jumping off a bridge that wasn't too far from where they were.

"Don't cry for her," the evangelist said, 'someday, you'll find someone better. Let me share something much more important with you...', and he proceeded to share with him about the gospel.

The young man decided to give his life and heart to Jesus that day. Victor had a Gideon's New Testament with him, which he gave to the boy; he didn't expect to see him again and soon forgot about him.

Many times as we work in missions, serving the Lord, we don't see the fruit of the seeds we've sown. But occasionally, there is an exception to that rule, in which God allows us the great privilege of seeing that fruit grow and sow its own seeds. This was the case with this young would-be suicide. After about twenty years of walking through that coffee field, Victor was invited to participate in some conferences in Medellin. He arrived late, and as he walked into the conference room as discreetly as he could, his arrival was announced by the main speaker, not to embarrass but to honor. They all gave him a general greeting, and the conference continued. After Victor had found his seat, suddenly, a hand came from behind and rested on his shoulder. Looking back, Victor saw a man with an elegant haircut and a large mustache,

"Brother Victor," the man said, "how are you?" Victor could not hide his awkwardness before the realization that he could not recognize the man greeting him. "It was in Segovia," the man continued to refresh his memory, "I was crying about ..." he wasn't able to finish as Victor interrupted him excitedly,

"About you getting dumped by your girlfriend! And I gave you a News Testament, right?" They both laughed together as they went over the old but good memory and caught up on each other's lives.

"So what do you do now?" Victor asked. The answer moved Victor deeply.

"I'm a pastor, and I have a beautiful congregation. So I really wanted to thank you personally after all these years."

This is the evangelist's life; he has good and bad news to tell. But in the end, all works for good. What marks the difference in all of this is having the ongoing company of the Holy Spirit, which produces joy, even in the most bottomless hole that there may be. This life is to be walked, led by the hand of God as we co-create with Him. He is joyful to take us to places where no one else has gone before to share His Good News.

Fruit and Stones

7

"Why are they holding white handkerchiefs? Is there a member of the government coming to visit today? Is the president coming?" These were the questions going through Victor's head as he, upon a horse, and accompanied by several other Christians, rode into a small village in the province of El Choco.

Some months after his episode with the young man in the coffee field, Victor received a three-day invitation to organize an evangelistic campaign in this remote village. Just to arrive there, he and his company had to ride horseback for about six hours in a torrential rainstorm.

As they arrived, a great multitude came to receive them; they were mostly adults. They positioned themselves on either side of the main road. They were all very excited; they had white handkerchiefs in their hands, which they waved in the air above their heads. They gave shouts full of joy and emotion as the company drew near. As Victor asked his guide why they were so happy, he began to understand the depth of their situation.

It wasn't governors, politicians, presidents, or media celebrities who were the object of such a joyous welcome. The Christians who lived in that town had come to know Jesus through radio programs broadcasted by the Transmundial Radio Station, not through an evangelist or pastor. Therefore, their knowledge and experience of the Christian life had been somewhat limited. Not that one can't learn and experience Jesus by oneself. Still, Jesus tends to enjoy showing himself through others whose desire is to conform to His image.

"They're welcoming you," said the guide. "It's been so many years since they've had to chance of receiving a preacher amongst them."

There were hundreds of people, and they insisted that Victor start teaching that very day in four different services – to which he immediately and gleefully agreed.

Victor had many new experiences through the hospitality he received in this town, which brought comfort to his heart and rest to his body. One of them was, very simply put: the bed. It was allegedly the best bed in the whole town. It resembled a wooden box, filled to about half a meter with bean husks. Even today, he says, "In my whole life, before or since, I've never felt such a comfortable bed."

Victor taught and preached a lot for the next three days, so he became hoarse. At the end of his time there, he felt the Holy Spirit whispering to him:

"Well done, my son."

Many surrendered their lives to Jesus during those days; there was an exceptional harvest for the Kingdom of God. Even though he had no salary, savings, or constant financial support, Victor lacked nothing. Instead, he left the town with much more than he had arrived with.

Many people say: "I want to be an evangelist," "I want to be a pastor," and.... "How much does it pay?" Dear reader, if someone invites you somewhere to preach, evangelize, or somehow contribute to the Great Commission, whether it be in or out of your own country or continent, it is God who pays; and He pays best. So give it everything you have. The harvest is plentiful, but the laborers are few; we must cry out to the Lord of the harvest so that He will send more workers. God pays best, and He will take care of all your needs. Jesus tells us not to worry about what we will wear, dress or eat. We must focus on the Kingdom of God and His Righteousness; all else with be added. When we make God our absolute priority, we become free from any worry or concern about ourselves, and God gladly takes care of those concerns – much more efficiently than we can.

Even though the Bible talks about and promises affliction and persecution for God's people for the sake of Jesus, we can see the mercy of God in action in remarkable ways. In some cases, immediate persecution is avoided. Victor learned this first-hand in a small town not so far from where he was welcomed with white handkerchiefs. This town is called Cisneros. He went there to organize a Christian parade through town. This mission was highly impactful since Cisneros was a town riddled with anti-Christian sentiment and propaganda. In preparation for this parade, flags, posters, and banners were made. While Victor was having a look at them, a man with a stern but respectful expression came up to him. He turned out to be the Colonel who resided in that area.

"Are you planning on doing a Christian march or something?" he asked with concern. "That is not a custom that would be smiled upon around here. In fact, no one has ever done it, and all you should expect would be a constant rain of fruit and stones coming at you from the buildings on the side of the road. Plus, a lot of abusive language would be thrown your way."

Victor explained that they were just being obedient to God, and therefore they had no plan B. The only thing they would do about it was to pray for protection the night before the march. Amongst those that went to pray that night, there was an elderly woman of about sixty years of age approximately. She turned out to be none other than the Colonel's mother. Victor found this whole situation quite comical. He could barely hold in his laughter when he heard that she had forced her son – the Colonel – to send a small contingent to personally guard and protect the Christians as they carried out their march for Jesus. Guards were posted at the front and back of the multitude. Many came out of their houses to observe the "evangelicals." Some joined in with the singing and shouts of praise. Others became very angry at the sight of the march. Still, they couldn't take any action, thanks to the company of soldiers that protected the Christians. As they marched through town under the bright sun, they gave out tracts to whomever they saw. Victor never forgot the two people in the front row of the march: The Colonel and his mother.

Nowadays, considering how the economy is headed, the most seen poster outside factories, businesses, and enterprises are "No vacancies." People are getting laid off right and left. But the only place where there are always vacancies is the largest multinational company in the whole world, which has representatives in every nation on earth; The Kingdom of God. He always has vacancies, and He is seeking for workers to be part of His Kingdom. Victor is one of those workers, and The Lord also has a very special position reserved just for you. So let us work together for the best boss, friend, and Father: God Almighty.

The Ship and the Woman in White

8

The night was cold, but the thick country blankets put up quite a defense. Although animal shrieks and insect chatter constantly interrupted the nightly silence, Victor's sleep was deep due to physical exhaustion. Yet, despite his weariness, there was a smile of satisfaction on his face for the work that had been done. Five years had already passed since Victor had his dramatically profound encounter with The Lord on the day he planned to commit suicide. It had been five years of evangelism, church planting, and learning to trust in God for his provision and countless miracles. Victor didn't know it at the time, but all this was a part of God's special training for a very special and unique job He had for Victor in the future, a job that Victor couldn't even remotely imagine at the time.

That night, overcome with the need to rest, he lay in bed after an intense and long evangelical campaign in Segovia, Antioquia. Then, finally, Victor succumbed to sleep. Instantly he saw himself wearing an exquisitely elegant white suit as he walked up the ramp of an immense transatlantic cruise ship. Once on the deck, he immediately saw three men approaching him with a very firm stride. They all wore formal and distinct uniforms; two wore the same kind; they were sailors. They escorted the third on either side, which was obviously a higher-ranked man, who Victor assumed to be the cruiser's Captain.

"Welcome, Victor; the table is ready for you. Please follow me and take a seat."

They led him to a long rectangular table on the ship's deck. Laid out in front of him was the most extravagant banquet he had ever laid eyes on. Victor saw all kinds of meats, including many he had never seen before. There were different cuts of turkey, chicken, roast beef, smoked pork, slices of ham, beautiful cuts of bacon, and all kinds of sausages. There were many types of bread; French, Arab, and many others. These were decorated with as many different kinds of cheeses and beverages as one could imagine. It was such a splendid sight that anyone would have questioned the reliability of their eyes.

Victor took the seat he was led to by the Captain. As he sat down, the sound of mighty thunder cracked through the sky far away. Looking up, he saw how the clouded sky opened before his eyes, revealing blinding rays of light that reached the horizon. Then he heard nothing other than the audible voice of the Lord:

"Victor, I want you to come with me to China..."

Victor was an evangelist; he had never considered himself a missionary because even though he had gone to many towns and cities, he had never left his own country. So the Lord's words surprised him, as he had never set his eyes on China, and he didn't know much about Asia either.

"And I'm going to take you there once you are married," God continued, and then He said something that really got Victor's attention, "I will take you once you're married."

Suddenly, before Victor's eyes appeared a beautiful woman in a wedding dress white as snow. He could see that she was obviously from a foreign country. Her hair was as blonde as could be, her skin white, and her eyes clear blue. Those were the only aspects he could define about her because, for some bizarre reason, God did not allow him to clearly see her face. Whenever he tried to focus on her whole face to get a mental picture to remember, her face became completely blurry. The more he tried to see her face, the blurrier she became. Finally, all he heard was God's voice:

"This is your wife," said The Lord.

Victor woke up sweating, speechless, and stupefied by the dream. He had recently been praying for a wife; he thanked God for giving him the answer.

With no further questions, he knelt next to his bed, and from that morning forward, he started to pray, intercede, and fast for China. He sought sources of information concerning China, which wasn't the easiest of tasks in 1976. He could not access the Internet in those days and had no subscription to National Geographic. He decided to find missionaries from the United States of America; he thought they would at least have some useful information about China. However, on hearing about his desire to go to Asia, they answered,

"How do you think you'll be able to go to China? You are Colombian and don't have the money for those kinds of trips. So maybe God gave you that dream to tell you to pray for China; 'cause you don't have the money for missions."

These were good people; they opened schools and planted churches, but maybe they lacked belief in miracles or the fact that the Lord speaks through dreams in modern times. Victor learned through this that there were two types of missionaries. He who is immersed in the battlefield and has had to learn to live by faith or retreat; and he who feels more comfortable behind a desk and from there he seeks strategies for fund-raising. Despite the words from these missionaries, Victor's conviction was not shaken. Deep down in his being, he knew that the Lord had called him to go to China because the Holy Spirit constantly reminded him of this.

Victor started to spend many hours of intense prayer for China. He would visualize himself in the Eastern Giant, in a future that, in his imagination, was pretty close; he estimated that he would be there in six months. Little did he know that fourteen years would go by before the dream would become a reality.

Youth With A Mission

9

In the Old Testament, the Lord took the Israelites from Egypt into the desert for forty years to change their selfish character and their slave mentality into a mindset in which they realized they were the people of God. When that change occurred, and the old patterns, habits, and lifestyle were dead, they were ready to enter the Promised Land. Hundreds of years later, before the simple shepherd was crowned as king, David was led into exile; here, God taught him a lifestyle of war in which he would learn to either depend on the Lord or fail and most surely die. The Lord had shown Victor His plan for taking him to China, and He desired that Victor succeed in his mission. The next essential step would be to mold him in the school of humility. The mold to be used for this purpose was the international missionary organization Youth With A Mission, more known by its initials: YWAM.

One night Victor received a dream from the Lord with some precise instructions:

"Drop your role as a pastor, and join Ywam."

Ywam is a missionary organization founded by Loren Cunningham in 1960 and now spreads all over the globe. As Victor arrived at the Ywam center in Bogota, he saw it was full of young people; young people like him; passionate for the Lord with the desire to do evangelism and discipleship whenever the opportunity presented itself and wherever God should lead them. It was an entirely voluntary movement, and those who were a part of it depended utterly on the Lord's provision. Victor would learn to do the same to pay for his DTS (Discipleship Training School), which lasted five months. Then he would continue trusting in the Lord to continue to pay the staff fee every month, which would cover basic living expenses such as water, gas, food, and electricity.

With all his previous experience as an evangelist and pastor, being in Ywam was a challenge to his pride. Being a man who had led many campaigns and other significant Christian events, he thought that upon arrival in his DTS, he would be instructed in the essential arts of cross-cultural missions, and from there on, his time would be dedicated to entirely to the mission field. So he surely felt a strange mix of emotions and feelings when he was assigned the daily duty of cleaning the bathrooms on his first day.

Many years were spent in this process of growing in the knowledge of the Lord and making Him known to others side-by-side with other passionate men and women of God. But the road would be challenging because the Lord was committed to changing aspects of Victor's character. If left unchecked, these aspects would be a stumbling block to himself and others.

On one particular occasion, some time after having entered Ywam, a young man came knocking on the base's front door. The man in charge of answering it that week was soon looking for Victor.

"Brother," he said when he found him, "someone is looking for you at the door. He says he needs to speak about an urgent matter."

As Victor went to see who his visitor was, he recognized a young man who had worked with him when he used to be a pastor.

"Victor!" said the young man with a great smile, "we would love to have you lead an evangelism campaign this weekend! Can you come?"

Victor said yes; it had been so long since he had led an evangelism campaign of this magnitude.

Without allowing anything to distract him, Victor ran straight to the office where his leaders were to give them the news about his new weekend plans. He needed to go and pack immediately and go with his friend to make preparations.

"But Victor," they said to him with slight confusion written on their faces, "aren't you on reception duty this weekend? You must stay here to answer the telephone and keep guard while everyone else goes home.... Did you forget?"

Victor didn't expect this answer, and in his excitement about the prospect of campaigning for Jesus, he had forgotten entirely that he was assigned that weekend for reception duty. He realized he wouldn't have any permission to abandon his duty. Pride and indignation welled up inside of him. His anger was so that he marched out of that office without another word; he packed his bags and simply left. He spent two months away from Ywam, pastoring and campaigning. And frankly, as he said himself, it all went terribly for him. The Lord's blessing was not upon him, and he knew it.

He returned to Ywam broken, humbled, and with tears in his eyes. He asked God - and his mentors - to forgive him for His disobedience and desire to be independent. He was received back home with arms open wide. Of course, he was completely forgiven.

On another occasion, the desire to leave Ywam once again surfaced. So he packed his bags and secretly took them to his mother's house. No one knew about his intentions about leaving. He returned to pick up a pair of dirty socks that he'd left behind. He said to himself,

"I'll wash these socks, hang them out to dry, and get out of here; I'm tired of this! I don't need these people! Why should I submit to them?"

Needless to say, Victor's pride was getting the best of him. He thought it was enough for God to speak to him; the time of taking orders from mere mortals ended. But his best friend Cristo Manuel approached him as we washed his socks. And Cristo Manuel had a very strong prophetic gifting.

"What's going on, Victor J?"

Cristo Manuel always called him with a "J," which was his middle initial - for Julio. Cristo reached into his pocket and took out his harmonica, and began to play it and sing a song in the vallenato style that went as follows:

Victor,

Why do you want to leave Ywam, son?

> Why do you go as if hiding?
> Without the guidance of the Lord... Ay 'ombre! It will not go well for you;
> The Lord says you should stay, man, And He will bless you;
>
> And He'll take you to China, ay' ombre!

Victor turned pale. He was speechless while his jaw hung low. Cristo Manuel must have thought he was merely making up some improvised, funny, random song. But Victor knew it was a message from God directly for him.

"How did he know?" Victor asked himself as he went to his room to kneel down and repent of his decision to leave. "How did he figure me out?"

He was back at his mother's home, picking up his bags in no time. He quietly returned them to the Ywam base without making it too public. He once again submitted to the covering of his leaders; God kept him in Ywam Bogota for many more years. Victor attempted to leave the Ywam community on three occasions, but God had placed him there in the first place to strengthen his character. He learned to depend on the Holy Spirit for everything, from an airplane ticket, even down to a razor blade.

We can see this method of God working in the character of His children. We can see it in the life of Joseph. Maybe he became proud because God revealed himself to him through dreams. Therefore, the Lord had to take him to Egypt as a slave and then live as a prisoner; all to learn humility. Only after this challenging time was God able to promote him to be the second most powerful man in the whole kingdom of Egypt.

So, my dear reader, don't be too rushed to be the 'best,' or to have the most extraordinary ministry, or to make the 'biggest' impact, because the most critical requirements for the work and walk with God are a simple humility and dependence on the Holy Spirit. The most important things for Him are our heart and character, not our abilities or giftings. If we are humble and obedient, the Lord will take us soon enough to wherever it is He has called us. So the only question that remains is, what are we focusing on more: on developing our gifting or abiding in Jesus?

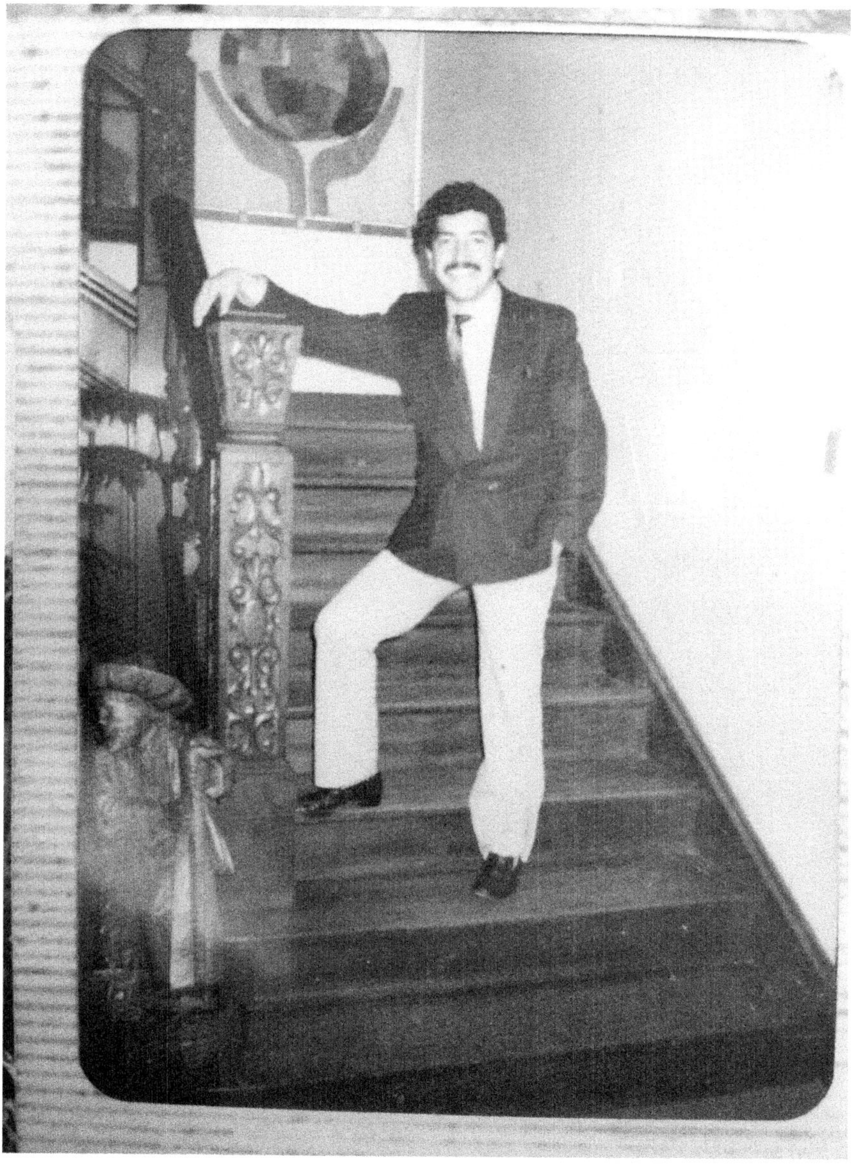

His Money
His Time
His Strength

10

    Victor sat on his bed in his dear mother's house. The last thing he wanted at the moment was to talk with anybody. Maybe it was the shame or a feeling of guilt. Perhaps the lying thought accused him of somehow failing his leaders, his friends, and those who admired him and had been praying for his calling to China.

    "What had happened? I was supposedly meant to be in China right at this moment. They prayed for me so much – and I failed! Did I muddle up my calling? Did I misunderstand the calling in itself?" – there was an orchestra of questions, doubts, and frustrations playing a thunderous and dark melody in the thoughts of the Colombian missionary.

    Only a couple of months before, he was more than convinced of shortly living in China, working hand-in-hand with God to save lost souls. Sitting on his bed, as he unpacked his bags, he meditated on what had happened.

    Those were the days when Billy Graham was carrying out a lot of programs to train other evangelists to be better equipped and more passionate about sharing the Good News. Mr. Graham organized a congress in the Netherlands to which he invited many evangelists and pastors from all over the world; for many, he even paid their flights, housing, and food expenses. Victor was one of these invited guests. As part of the trip, an additional opportunity presented itself for Victor during his time in Europe. Victor had some studies in communications, which enabled him to have his own radio programs with a Godly message during his years as an evangelist. He was recognized by many all around Colombia for his radio messages. Some friends presented a proposition to him: that after the conference, he should visit them, he would get a secure job with them on a European radio channel; then he could fill his pockets with money and go to China with those earnings in no time.

Needless to say, the idea caught Victor's attention, being aware that it would be harder by any normal means to get the necessary finances to go to China, being in Colombia. So, before leaving the country, all the Ywamers in Bogota – about sixty in total – met together for a grand celebration as a farewell for Victor, the missionary towards the Eastern Giant. They blessed him with financial offerings and gifts, prayed for him, and celebrated that he was so close to the vision God had given him so many years ago.

Of course, there were tears as well when the goodbyes were said. Still, Victor left with a massive smile on his face as he walked through the boarding gate of the International Airport of Bogota without a hint of what awaited him in the following weeks.

Victor now neared the airport in Amsterdam after flying for approximately twelve hours. When his flight was about to touch down, Victor had a terrible clear feeling in his heart. He heard a very subtle voice that told him:

"The doors are closing, Victor."

He didn't like what he heard, nor did he like what he immediately started to feel. These words provoked an increased level of nervousness, which sent chills up and down his spine. For some reason, he couldn't help but be convinced about two single facts: first, he couldn't find any employment opportunities in Europe; second, he wouldn't be stepping onto Chinese ground on this trip as he had planned.

Billy Graham's conferences were, simply put, a resounding success. Everyone received priceless training for their respective ministries. In addition, groups of Christians from all around the world attended: Colombians, English, Indians, and Nigerians, among many others. It was all a small foretaste of heaven, being in such a great gathering amongst so many different nationalities and ethnic groups praising the Lord with their own gifts.

During the last days of the conference, tour groups were organized to see the world-famous capital of France – Paris. Victor decided to join one of these groups. His idea was to take advantage of the situation to get in touch with the radio station where he had been promised a 'stable job with great pay .'Once in Paris, he went to find a public phone box. During the call, the feeling and subtle voice he had heard and felt on the plane were proven true - he was informed that all those in charge of the radio station had very recently left for holidays. They wouldn't be available for the next month or two. The doors were closed entirely. The final verdict came on the other end of the line: "Victor, we recommend you go back to Colombia, and if you wish to return after a month or two, feel free to do so."

Once back from Paris, Victor walked the streets of Amsterdam with his head held low. There were tears in his eyes, frustration and anger in his blood - boiling up with every second that passed. Then, finally, he looked up and complained to his Father.

"You didn't help me! You closed the doors for me; I'm going to look so ridiculous going back to Colombia like this... You surely don't love me, and you know what? That's it! I'm NOT going to China!" These words came out with tears and anger towards God from the depths of his frustration, intending to exact revenge on the Lord.

Once his vengeful arsenal of complaints had subsided and the silence took over, he heard the voice of the Lord as clear as water. It was a tender voice, very different from that of the missionary. It was gentle as if unaffected by the accusations and complaints - although doubtless, He had heard them all. Here came the question:

"Are you still angry, Victor?"

"Yes, Lord, I am"

"Son, you're frustrated and angry because the doors are closed. And it's all due to a mistake you made."

"What might that be?" Victor replied.

"Up to now, you have tried to go to China with your money, in your time, and with your strength. So go back to Colombia, son. For when I take you to China, it will be with My money, in My time, and with My strength."

These words were much more than a swift and firm correction from the Lord; they were actually a message of love, encouragement, and a statement of mercy since God actually explained the reason for what was happening to Victor at the time - something that the Lord is never obliged to do.

Upon Victor's return to Colombia, he struggled with shame, afraid that his Ywam family would see him after his "failure in Europe ."The shame was so much that he didn't let anyone in Ywam know about his situation. Instead, he quietly went straight to his mother's home to be with his family. In a way, he was hiding. As he sat on his bed, all these memories, questions, and doubts rolled through his mind. The orchestra in his head was a dark mist that clouded and blinded the natural eye, but the bright and powerful light of God broke through with the phrase he had heard in Amsterdam:

"I'll take you to China; with My money, in My time, and with My strength."

By some strange means, but probably through word of mouth as tends to happen, the Ywamers heard about what had happened to Victor - and like good South Americans, they simply came to visit him unannounced. Their grace, understanding, and unconditional friendship were such that Victor felt the shame melt away. He felt free to return to the base and be with his brothers and sisters in ministry. Victor would continue to walk in obedience to the Lord and take steps toward China in due time. This time he was conscious that the Lord would take him there, with His money, in His time, and with His strength.

Your God will be my God

11

As the years in Ywam went by, Victor took every opportunity that was given to him to share about the vision the Lord had given him about China. Some said he was crazy, doubting God had ever spoken to him. But the Holy Spirit strengthened him by reminding him:

"Be calm, Victor. I called you, and I will take you. Don't doubt it."

These encouraging words kept him standing firm during the stronger attacks against his faith.

Victor was a man with a clear-cut call. To stay consistent with his calling for the rest of his life, he started to employ specific relational guidelines whenever they proved to be necessary. Victor was a man of a strong vision, faith, and a bachelor. Therefore, he sometimes attracted a certain level of attention from the opposite sex. Nevertheless, Victor knew he needed to marry the one the Lord had for him because together, they would walk in the vision God had given him long ago. So, whenever a young lady would show any interest in him, Victor would pop the question (yes, at the right time, and in the right way):

"Would you be willing to go to live in China?"

This directness would automatically have the tendency to discourage any romantic pursuit towards him.

However, one day, in 1987 - a year Victor would never forget - an exceptionally special someone arrived at the Ywam base in Bogota. She wasn't Colombian. She came from England, and although her real name was Margaret, everyone knew her by Peggy (and many believed her real name was Peggy, including her son until the age of thirteen). In England, she had worked in social work and then received the vision from the Lord to become a missionary. She spent $2\frac{1}{2}$ years in Israel, where God spoke to her about going to South America. She chose to go with Ywam and did her basic training (DTS) in Scotland in 1985. Peggy experienced the joy and honor of meeting extraordinary people and developing deep friendships that would undoubtedly last a lifetime. As enjoyable and enriching as that was, she had also had to experience the emotional strain of continually making friends and then saying goodbye to these friends as she moved from one outreach or training course to another. This had happened over and over.

One evening at a large conference for women intercessors, Lydia, the speaker, was giving specific words to specific individuals, words from God. Peggy was exhausted; all were singing the last song when suddenly God spoke to her, "Wake up, Peggy, I'm going to speak to you." Wow! The song finished, and the speaker said, "There's one more person who needs a word from God, and it's this: ask whatever you want, and I'll give it to you."

Awed at the directness and intimacy of this moment with God, Peggy felt free to open her heart and think of what she really wanted. Wisdom, like Solomon? No, with all the traveling and changes, what she wanted was settled: the stability and security of human love - a husband. The conversation with God all happened so simply. In her mind, she said, "I want a missions husband."

"When you get to South America, you'll find your husband there." He replied.

So, she got her visa as soon as possible! She packed her bags and headed off to Colombia, where a ministry of Ywam was working with street children. She arrived at the Ywam base in Bogota, the only Colombian base at that time, and had brought along an excellent camera, which the ministry leaders thought would be a great instrument to raise awareness about the poorest areas of the city - namely, La Calle del Cartucho. She agreed to the photography project.

Her task was to take pictures of the houses, the people, the children, and the faces of the inhabitants of the streets. However, el Cartucho was also known for being a dangerous and lawless place. And to send an obvious foreigner all by herself would've been downright foolish - so the base leaders started searching for a bodyguard from amongst the men of the base who would be willing to get up in the early hours of the morning to accompany her. She insisted this was not necessary, but the leaders insisted more.

The leaders approached Victor,

"Son, would you consider being Peggy's bodyguard while she carries out her photo project?"

This didn't appeal to the seasoned evangelist at first since it implied waking up at 4:30am every day for the whole week (and it's not like he would get the chance to go to sleep any earlier). So the leaders looked around for someone else who might step up to the task, but they came back with nothing. So finally, they had no choice but to insist that Victor do it, and he finally agreed.

The next day, a little after four o'clock in the morning, Victor was woken by repeated knocking on his door.

"Victor, are you up yet?"

He had overslept. He quickly got out of bed, tidied himself up, and walked into the dining room to find a full hot breakfast served and waiting for him on the table. "No woman (other than Mother) has ever prepared breakfast for me before," he thought to himself.

Through this project, they got to know each other better. The photography progressed, and they enjoyed the breakfasts they shared more and more. To begin with, the project was only meant to last for a week, but somehow it rolled on into a whole month. They enjoyed spending all this time together. And as expected in any community - especially in a Latin community - many people started talking about the two who were spending a lot of time on a "simple" task. Did they have discernment? Or did they just have a gift for being suspicious?

The day came when one of the base leaders, during a time of community intercession, stood up and said loud and clear for all to hear,

"I feel from the Holy Spirit that we must pray for a wife for Victor."

Some had trouble holding in the crack of laughter; others just looked at Victor and gave him a cheeky smile. Victor was sure that this was all a big joke from everyone, but he had to smile as his eyes began to close and prayer started rising to heaven. And as an answer to those prayers, something quite peculiar happened. That same week Peggy found herself trying to lift up a heavy and wide box full of videotapes (if you're born after '95, just think Big Box full of Netflix subscriptions) to place it in the upper compartment of a tall closet. She wasn't getting too far. When she looked around to see if anyone could help her, guess what? Yep, you guessed it; Victor was there, just walking by. He came to her rescue (try to imagine this in slow motion) and lifted the box over his head. Then he turned his face towards Peggy as if to say something; he froze. It was as if his eyes had been opened for the first time. She was absolutely stunning.

From there, they started to spend more time together. Eventually, they presented their relationship formally to the leadership of the base. Most of the leadership agreed that this relationship was from God, and they celebrated it. As a result, the young couple (both being thirty-four years of age) had the chance to get to know each other a lot better and grow in admiration for each other grounded in their love and commitment to Jesus over the coming season.

There are seasons and times in our walk with God when we can feel tired, on the verge of being worn out – even bored. Then, the Lord can give us a chance for short or long-term change to "recharge" our batteries. Victor was tired, feeling stuck, and sometimes found himself playing with God's anointing and principles. Sometimes old thoughts came to visit him, the voices that told him that it would be better for him to go home, to leave Ywam; he didn't need to submit to those leaders. But God had plans of His own for Victor, and therefore, Victor had a dream. In this dream, God himself asked him a question.

"What would you like me to do for you, son?"

"Bless me," he answered, "I'm bored; take me to a place where there's been no preaching before. I'm bored in Colombia."

Not four hours had passed since Victor woke up from this dream that the leaders called Victor to their office to talk. They were looking for someone who would like to go to Peru to organize a sizable evangelistic event.

"We have chosen you and your friend Cristo Manuel to go and open the way in Lima and Cusco, the spiritual capital of the Incas."

"Wow! He only took three hours on this one," Victor exclaimed on the inside. He could see that soon he would be leaving for Peru, so he invited Peggy for a special lunch that would change everything. Peggy was surprised upon arriving - it was a Chinese restaurant. They went in and sat at the table and chatted until the waiter trotted along to take their order, but Victor signaled for him to wait a few more minutes.

"Peggy," he said, directing his attention back to her, "Do you like this restaurant? Does it catch your eye?"

"Yes, I do," she answered, "but why have you brought me to a Chinese restaurant?"

"I've already told you a couple of times about what God has spoken to me concerning China and my calling to go there. So, I wanted to ask you," - there was a pause - "Would you like to come to China with me... as my wife?"

That was the critical question, and he had thrown it out there. The answer would define whether or not Peggy and Victor would go together to China, and he would keep on being her bodyguard for the rest of their lives. His question caught her off guard, but her answer surprised him even more.

"Give me five minutes to think about it," and she bowed her head to pray in silence.

"Five minutes?" - he thought to himself - "WOW!" But after only three minutes, she looked up, straight at him with a gleaming smile.

"If you go to China, I want to go with you. Your people will be my people, and your God will be my God."

"Now you may bring the food out!" the newly engaged man shouted out for all to hear in the restaurant.

At last, he had found the woman in white, which he had seen thirteen years ago in the dream of the Great Ship. He had found the woman of his dreams. He had found his wife. So, with peace and certainty that Peggy was the wife God had prepared for him - and the woman for whom he had been prepared - in

September of 1987, Victor and Cristo Manuel set out on their journey to Peru. The Lord blessed them and allowed them to prosper in the assignment they had been sent there to do, despite all the demonic opposition. There was no lack of resistance; there was reputation of a large population of practitioners of the occult who lived in that land. The spiritual capital of the Incas was there. So, the job was challenging, but up until today, Cristo Manuel and Victor remain the best of friends.

Victor would maintain communication with his fiancé mainly through letters; such letters became a treasure for him. In January of 1988, Victor wrote a letter that ended with the phrase: "If you come to Peru, we can get married in Cusco." And Peggy did just that; very soon, she was on her way there.

At the wedding, most of the guests were Ywamers and people who Victor had come to know in one of the various evangelistic trips in the last couple of months. The wedding was, for many, a golden closure for the outreaches carried out. Among the guests was Dorothy Churchill, Peggy's mother, who had come all the way from England to present this most important of events. The location chosen for the ceremony and reception was a beautiful whitewashed hotel outside Cusco in the steep-sided valley of Urubamba. The air was cold, but the sun shone throughout the whole wedding upon the bride and groom, the guests, and the astonishing mountain range that filled the horizon. There were moments of laughter throughout the wedding. Since Peggy didn't understand Spanish that well, she had to ask Victor to signal her the time to say 'I do' and then kiss to seal the ceremony. There was a great party and celebration that day. Many close friends, who displayed all their love and appreciation for them, surrounded the newlyweds on that lovely afternoon.

"I'll never forget it. That day brought great joy into the rest of my life", says Victor many times when remembering it. As they started on the journey to the airport to head on to their next destination – their honeymoon – they ran into many Ywamers who were also now traveling back to their own families or on holiday. Cristo Manuel was there and decided to go with the newlywed couple on the same plane – in the seat next to them! Needless to say, for a British person such as Peggy, this presented a substantial culture-shock moment. They sat with Cristo Manuel for the entire flight, and obviously, a lot of chatting went on between Victor and his best friend. When they landed, Cristo Manuel mentioned the possibility of staying in the same hotel as them. So they lost him as soon as they went through customs.

They spent their honeymoon at Lake Titicaca, traveling through Peru, Ecuador, and Colombia. After this, they returned to Ywam. The leaders asked Victor to consider being the permanent director for the missionary base in Peru. Victor submitted the option in prayer, but to his surprise, the Holy Spirit warned him against accepting their offer.

"I told you a long time ago that once you were married, I would take you to China, and now you're married. So get ready because very soon you'll depart."

Victor repented before the Lord, for he had forgotten about that specific aspect of the vision. So, with much gratitude, he respectfully declined the leaders' offer. They accepted his decision, knowing that the Holy Spirit was guiding the family. They blessed the new family and encouraged them to fix their direction hard like stone on the Eastern Giant. It turns out that within a year, they would be living in the People's Republic of China.

Victor and Peggy

You will cry in China

12

Victor remembered his failed attempt to go to China some years ago; he remembered the tears, the complaints, the despair, and the sweet words from his heavenly Father. These memories caused a great smile to spread across his face as he sat in the 747 Boeing en route to Hong Kong. Hong Kong is a part of China, but in those days, it had its own governing body, which enabled it to be the closest island to which a foreigner could process a visa to the interior of the Eastern Giant. In Hong Kong, Victor, Peggy, and other missionaries would wait to be launched into the heart of communist China.

The waiting period there was short, and a mush of different activities included waiting for visas, studying about the culture they were about to walk into, and learning as much as possible of the mainland Chinese language - Mandarin. Long meetings were held to pray - everyone joined joyfully, knowing they would soon be launched into the heart of China. Many were unaware of the giants they would soon be standing up to for the following years to come. Finally, the day came when they would have their last prayer meeting in Hong Kong. Soon they would cross the border. Victor and Peggy were present and full of expectations about hearing a special word from the Lord about their journey, something fundamental that they could anchor to and remember as they passed through the storms that lay ahead.

During this time of prayer, a prophet approached Victor. She was an older woman of short stature, with all her years engraved on the wrinkles on her smiling face. Yet, despite her elderly age, she evidently had a special and undeniable spirit of a warrior close to God's own heart, from whom she drew her strength.

"Victor," she said, looking at him straight in the eyes. "I have a message for you from the Lord."

The Colombian missionary's ears at once blocked out any noise other than the prophets' words. What did the Lord want to share with him? What secrets were about to be revealed that would imply total success for the missionary journey in China? So he was startled and taken aback by what the prophet had to say.

"I see you crying in China, Victor. I see your eyes full of tears. For quite some time, the Lord has desired to remove a bad smell you have. The horrible smell of pride, and in all these years, it has not departed you. He will take away this smell through your Mandarin language study."

Victor didn't give a high value to the prophet's words. He might have slightly believed it, but he didn't give it the seriousness such a message demanded. So along with Peggy and the other twelve missionaries, Victor embarked on the journey to Mainland China. He went as God had promised him some years ago; with His money, in His time, and in His strength. Soon they would be arriving at Chengdu - the city of the Panda - in the province of Sichuan in the center of China. In the year of Victor and Peggy's arrival in Chengdu - 1989 - Chengdu had a humble population of 1.8 million. In 2014 over 6.5 million people lived there, making it one of China's central and most commercial cities, a center for business, education, and politics.

On arrival, the missionaries learned that they had little freedom concerning their choice of where to stay. They couldn't just stay at any hotel they wished to. Most foreigners in China were restricted to staying only at the university accommodation specially set apart for foreigners. China was completely different in those days than it is now. Not even the biggest supermarkets had such things as cheese, nappies (diapers, yo), marmalade, jam, hamburgers, or french fries. Obviously, there was no knowledge of South American or Colombian food such as arepas or empanadas (tough to even get these today). The communist government had made sure to deport anything they considered a foreign influence. It was the first time they had seen dogs hanging in the marketplace right next to the pork and beef section - without mentioning the spicy seafood grills, commonly cluttered with hungry customers. The most common form of transportation was the bicycle, and there were only a handful of 'Western' toilets in the city - which weren't the first choice of the Chinese citizens.

As they arrived, the group of foreigners took only a short time to find the university where they would be learning Mandarin for most of their stay in China. A man from the admin department of the university showed them the way to their respective rooms. Upon seeing their rooms, the foreigners saw that there weren't any private bathrooms; they would have to use the communal bathrooms - shared with all the habitants of the building. This implied a cold walk down the stairs of the building, followed by making your way through a layer of snow that was a few feet deep during the winter - only to get to the restroom. They took the issue up to the directive of the university. They finally came to an agreement in which they would have their own bathrooms - at a higher cost. But at least each family would have their own restroom. After this, the foreigners settled in and quickly became friends with the local Chinese and Tibetans.

Sichuan province is considered to have one of the highest consumption of hot chilies - not to mention they are the spiciest ones by reputation. So whenever the foreigners were invited into the house of a Chinese or Tibetan friend, it would be normal for their faces to become red, sweaty, and contorted, with a lot of coughing, abusive use of napkins, and downing full glasses of water while having lunch or dinner. Teary eyes were not unusual (these weren't tears of joy or conviction). In many restaurants, there was no dish on the local menus that wouldn't cause them to start sweating - so they devised a plan. As Victor and Peggy developed a friendship with the owner of a restaurant, they gave her the "grand" idea to make "Chips-a" (French fries). This idea sounded really strange to the little lady, but it turned out to be a total success; that became the first restaurant in Chengdu to serve this "Western innovation."

Everyone was very excited and motivated to begin their classes of Mandarin. Classes began, and the Europeans, who by nature or nurture are gifted in language learning, began acquiring the basics of Mandarin in a matter of weeks. As they progressed, the prophet's words in Hong Kong became an evident reality in Victor's everyday life and studies. The professor at the university used English to explain the exercises to be done and the homework to be presented, but Victor didn't even understand English that well.

You must understand that shame played an important part in education in the Chinese culture of those days; sometimes, nowadays. It can be used as a mechanism of motivation or correction, and Victor's Mandarin professor used it generously. He embarrassed Victor in class for being a poor student compared to the other students. His classmates saw this and didn't appreciate it. Soon enough, they approached the teacher with the direct request that he stop treating their Colombian friend this way because it wouldn't be good for the student's learning environment. The professor agreed, and the episodes of public embarrassment and criticism towards Victor ended. He hadn't signaled him out intending to hurt him or because he might have despised South Americans – it was just an aspect of the culture, part of his daily life; he was most likely raised this way as a child.

Many a time, Victor would leave the classroom during break times and walk around the university campus. Full of frustration and discouragement, he walked; with hot tears streaming down his face, he questioned the Lord; why couldn't he understand the basics of Mandarin? Why was the pronunciation so difficult for him? Why couldn't he even understand the prices in the supermarket? Why had the Lord brought him to China? Was it just to suffer or to take vengeance for his sinful youth? These questions and thoughts were piling up in his mind and coming out in his conversations with his Father. The Holy Spirit always reminded him with gentleness and love that he wasn't in the wrong place. He was exactly where the Father wanted him to be.

"Don't worry about the language, son. You're doing just fine."

This became a routine for Victor; to leave the classroom as if defeated, to hear the sweet voice of his Saviour, wipe the tears from his eyes, lift his head up, and go back to class.

Heart Surgery

13

In most of the American continent, an evangelist can organize an evangelistic campaign completely freely and receive a lot of support. This campaign would be supported by churches, Christian businessmen, government members and could last a few months. It could be carried out in churches in small towns and fill entire stadiums, touching the lives of thousands and thousands of people. Thousands – even millions would raise their hands during those months to make a confession of faith. Many new churches would be planted; Christian radio stations would be opened and funded; even casinos, nightclubs, and bars would be shut down. There could be an impact on a major scale.

As a wandering evangelist, Victor was used to seeing these kinds of results in Colombia. So he expected to see the same astronomical results in China.

"I'm going to conquer China for Christ" is the line of thought many Christians have when they go for the first time to Asia. Having that expectation, they end up hitting the proverbial wall. They see that the results are entirely the opposite of what they expected. The fruits are few; there is no immediate conversion of the masses. It's an uphill struggle to see the first convert come to Christ. Many enter into a battle with frustration and discouragement. Some even renounce going to China; they leave depressed and feel God abandoned them. Regrettably, some abandon their faith in its totality.

After a year and a half of living in Mainland China and learning Mandarin, Victor could not say that a single Chinese had given his or her life to the Lord by him. Frustration attacked him day and night in the deepest corners of his mind.

"I'm no good for this language! No one understands what I say! Did God make a mistake bringing me here?" Victor said as he poured tears out frequently before his Father. But God, being an expert in dealing with his children, kept on encouraging him, showing him that it was His will that he be in China. Then, one day He shared something with Victor that only a few have heard from the Lord in the quiet place during their missionary ventures:

"Victor, I don't bring my children here to transform China in a single blow." The Lord said it while sharing His broken heart for the lost, "Sometimes I'm here alone; I don't have many friends here. Thank you for coming and being with me in this beloved nation, my son."

During their first year in China, medical tests confirmed that Peggy was pregnant. The family was full of joy, and a feeling of celebration overcame them upon hearing the precious news. The doctors told them a little boy was on the way. Victor and Peggy started thinking about the name they would give the little man. As they were used to depending on the Lord for everything in their lives, they decided to seek His guidance for the boy's name before they looked in a name book. And it turned out that the Lord did have a name reserved for him. After two weeks of praying a lot about the baby's name, Victor received a dream from God. In the dream, he was next to Peggy in his mother's house in Bogota. The whole family was there; brothers and sisters; aunts and uncles; nephews and nieces. They were all celebrating because a baby had been born among them. Victor's older sister – Nubia – walked over to a gently rocking crib in the middle of the room. As she moved closer to the baby's face, she called him with the familiar playful voice a grown-up calls a baby:

"Baby Oscar, baby Oscar, how's the little boy doing?"

Victor woke up from the dream, sitting straight up in his bed. He knew what the boy's name was! His name was Oscar, and God himself named him. He was grateful for this quick reply to his and Peggy's prayers. But there was still a mountain to cross.

Convincing Peggy of the baby's name would prove to be more of a challenge than Victor could handle on his own. As she heard about the dream he'd had, her facial expression gave away the fact that she disagreed with the baby's name. Her objection confirmed it.

"It's not a biblical name, Victor," she argued.

Victor was left a little confused and with the only option of going to God and asking Him Himself to convince Peggy of the baby's name. Some nights later, Victor had another dream – but this dream was a divine comedy! In the dream, Victor and Peggy sat in bed on a Sunday morning as if reading the newspaper. But they didn't have a newspaper; instead, they had a baby in their arms – and not any normal baby. He was larger than either Victor or Peggy as he lay in their arms. He was about 50 years old – and they playfully smiled and talked in baby language to him.

This time Victor woke up with his mouth full of laughter. "What a strange dream!" he thought.

He immediately recognized the great man he and Peggy had been holding in their arms in the dream; It was none other than Oscar Golden – a famous singer amongst the South American youths of the sixties.

"Peggy! Wake up!" he rapidly told his wife about the dream. "His name is definitely Oscar."

This time her reaction was different:

"Yes, Victor;" she nodded with a smile, "his name is Oscar."

This response from Peggy was a motive of joy for Victor, but they still didn't know the meaning of the baby boy's name. Peggy had a name book, which a German couple gave them. They didn't need to choose a name anymore; they simply needed to know the meaning of 'Oscar,' which God himself had chosen for the boy. When they found the name, they were surprised by what they read: DIVINE SPEARMAN. They instantly understood that little Oscar would have a special calling on his life.

The due date was getting close. The doctors didn't want to risk the baby being overdue. Another foreign couple had lost their child the previous year by waiting too long. So they decided to induce the birth. But four days passed, and there was still no sign of the birth of the divine spearman wanted to shoot out. The doctors finally approached Peggy and said,

"If he isn't born tomorrow, we'll have to do it by C-section," the reason being the gynecologist had her holidays to go to.

This only brought more worry to the couple because an all-out surgery in 1990 in China would have been much riskier for both Peggy and Oscar than if it had been done in England; the recovery would definitely have been more uncomfortable for Peggy. But by God's hand, that same night, on the 21st of July of 1990, at 10:30, after a final attempt to provoke an induced delivery, Oscar was born.

Oscar's birth had a distinct and unique impact on Victor. He had always had trouble relating to the Lord in a father-and-son manner. It was hard for him to picture God as a personal and close Father – thanks in some way to his own childhood and youth, which had left some severe scars in his life. But when he saw his son in his arms – a little, fragile, and vulnerable Oscar – he felt a new love sprout inside him towards his son. He heard the Holy Spirit whisper to him:

"Victor, do you love Oscar?"

"Of course I do; I would give everything for him – to protect him," Victor replied.

"Well, Victor,' the Holy Spirit answered back. "I love you so much more than you could ever love Oscar; I'm going to use him to heal the wounds that have marked your heart for so many years."

This brought great encouragement to Victor, and he was able to start to develop a different sort of relationship towards the Lord, not so much the servant-master relationship, but more like the son-father one.

Despite all the joy surrounding him, little Oscar's welcoming into the real world wasn't without difficulty or harsh conditions. From the first day of his life, acute bronchitis was diagnosed in his body. This presented a threat to his young life, but thank God there was treatment for it in China at the time – although efficient, the remedy would be long and uncomfortable. Victor and Peggy had to take Oscar to the hospital three times a day for ten days to receive antibiotic injections to counteract the disease. After that, his life was able to continue – not without an irrational fear of injections (and of dogs for some reason) for many years to come.

Oscar's birth had brought about profound changes in Victor's heart. As a sailor stands in awe before the magnificence of an iceberg, even though he could only see a small portion of it, Victor was experiencing a small fraction of the love that the Lord had for him by the love he himself had for his son. Despite this revelation, the attacks of frustration and discouragement that came with living as a missionary in the Eastern Giant didn't cease. The constant lack of fruit; after a year and a half of living in China, there was not a single person that could say that Victor led them through the process of entering the kingdom of heaven. Victor complained in his heart. He had many tear-filled conversations while walking around the college campus during class breaks.

His internal conflict was escalating out of proportion to the point where the Lord gave him another dream with a very different message from any previous vision. In this dream, Victor found himself in an impeccable, white operating room. In the middle of this room, there was an operating table, upon which he saw a baby laying face up. Victor suddenly realized that there was a lot of desperate crying and screaming going on – and it was coming from the baby. The child violently kicked and wildly threw its arms in all directions; his behavior was so aggressive that he could have caused anyone to retreat – and the doctor wasn't an exception. The man in the room dressed in a white uniform and latex gloves went over to the baby boy, and it was evident to Victor that the child was indeed sick and in need of urgent surgery. The doctor tried to calm the baby; he tried to reason with him that everything was going to be ok - that it was all for his own good. But the baby's wailing was relentless. He screamed louder and louder. Finally, the doctor realized that he simply wouldn't be able to operate on the child. His eyes welled up with tears.

"I don't understand this; what does it mean? Who is this baby?" Victor asked.

"Victor, that baby is you. For a long time I have tried to heal you, to cut your pride away; it's one of the reasons I brought you to China. But even here, you constantly complain - desperately complaining to me because it hurts. So, son, I will have to pause the surgery."

Victor perfectly understood what the Lord was referring to. His own eyes filled with tears. He begged the Lord,

"Forgive me, Lord. I will stop complaining! Please continue the surgery, please." But Victor received his final verdict,

"No, son. We will take a rest. Keep calm, and we'll restart the surgery later."

From Heart to Heart

14

One day there was an urgent knock on the family's front door. On opening it, Victor found himself face to face with another Ywam missionary – James. James came from the Philippines, and as I write this, he remains in China – married to his Chinese wife. James entered the apartment to explain his situation to Victor. He had been testifying about Jesus for quite some time to a fellow classmate at the university. His name was Steven. He had been sharing the Gospel with him for over a year, but without him deciding to give his life to the Lord. James was getting quite desperate and with good reason. In about a week's time, Steven would be leaving the city to return home to work, which was hundreds of miles away from Chengdu. He"d probably never have the chance to hear the Gospel again.

This was, indeed, a matter of life or death; an eternal consequence was in play.

"Victor, please talk with him. You have more experience doing this than I do. Please, just speak with him!"

After explaining to James about his lack of fluency in Mandarin – James insisted nonetheless – Victor accepted. James set things up so that Steven would meet him to "practice English and Mandarin" together, hoping that they would develop a quick friendship in order for Victor to be able to speak to him about Jesus. After a day or so, they finally met. They played table tennis, walked, and ate noodles together. They had conversations that deepened until the point of reaching the eternal life subject. This they talked about for a few days regularly. On his last visit, Victor saw the opportunity to unload over Steven his arsenal of theological and philosophical weaponry that he had learned to master through many years of study and investigation, seminars, institutes, and Ywam. After what seemed like an hour of speaking to Steven non-stop, Victor's throat became dry; if there were any words left to say, they simply refused to come out. Like a boxer after a long fight, Victor was breathless, tired, and needed a break.

In that silence, Steven's response finally emerged.

"Victor, I really want to thank you – because I know you want to help me with your God. But let me tell you the truth..." there was a pause in which Steven sought to find the correct words to continue. "I don't really understand your Mandarin, Victor."

Those words felt like a punch below the belt, a sword through his spirit. All his years of theological seminaries in evangelism crumpled like toilet paper before Steven's simple but honest statement. Victor looked up to the sky, and without caring that Steven could hear or see him, he shouted in frustration.

"You didn't help me! I've been talking to this guy for over an hour straight, and he will go to the darkness because he doesn't understand my Chinese? This is *your* fault!"

Instantly, there was silence – a very intense silence, as if Victor's accusations still lingered in the atmosphere – the Lord then answered him gently, firmly, and full of love at the same time.

"Victor, Steven has been listening to philosophies his whole life under a communist order. He's lived without a father and has been oppressed and used by his own government as a cog. People have tried to force the communist philosophies down his ears since he was a small boy. He doesn't need to hear more philosophy or apologetics. You've been talking to his mind, from your mind. Speak to him, from heart to heart."

With tears in his eyes still, Victor looked at Steven with a new depth and a new understanding of his life that caused compassion to come forth in his heart and said:

"My friend, I know you've suffered and that your father wasn't good to you; I know he used to hit and beat you, and you never heard the words "I love you." Forgive me for not speaking good Chinese. But I just want to say one last thing to you: You have a Father in heaven who loves you with all his heart and died for you so that you could meet him."

Steven remained still, but his face became pale, and evidently, he didn't know where to look.

"Victor," he said abruptly with a shaky and hurried tone, "I've got to go! I'm sorry, but I've really got to go. Bye–bye!"

And with that, the young man turned around and hurriedly left. It all happened so fast that Victor had difficulty processing what had just happened.

"What happened? Did he not understand what I said? Your strategy didn't really seem to work, Jesus. He didn't say the *sinners' prayer*" – he conversed with his God in his spirit.

"Victor," the Lord answered, "believe it or not, that young man has just become your brother."

"Lord, that's impossible; he didn't say the sinner's prayer."

For years, his culture had taught him that salvation comes solely through a repeated prayer, which is conveniently done in less than a minute. Contrast that with the picture painted for us by the early church, where the Christians would stare death in the eyes, whether it would come at the hands of the Roman soldiers, Jewish Pharisees, or at the claws and fangs of the beasts of the coliseum, they would confess that "Jesus is Lord," knowing that their life on earth would be ended in an instant. The teaching of his culture is what created doubt in Victor's mind – "How could it be possible that he had become a believer without repeating *the sinners' prayer*?"

When he finally got back to his wife and son, he told Peggy about the events of the day.

"... But, he didn't repeat the confession of faith, honey." Victor continued his protest.

However, Peggy, coming from Europe, knew that God doesn't always maintain Himself aligned with the traditions and methods humans create and bestow upon Him – even in the church.

"But Victor," she replied him, "if the Holy Spirit told you that Steven became a Christian, then it's because it's true!"

Of course, she was right; and Victor accepted that. Without much delay, the following morning, there were hurried knocks on the family's front door. Victor rushed to see who it was.

"Hi, Puliwei (Victor's Chinese name)!" Steven greeted him with a huge smile and a lot of enthusiasm. "I also want to be a Christian, like yourself – and follow Jesus. Could you help me?"

"Come on in, buddy. Before you get cold."

That was the first fruit Victor saw in China, in which the Lord had given him the privilege of taking part in the reaping.

Victor continued developing relationships with his professors and student friends. One of the advantages of being a Latin-American was the cultural 'warmth' one brings, making it easier to win the affection and trust of others, in general. For example, Victor had a recurring Tibetan teacher; he was married and had a beautiful family. Let's say his name was John, and he was one of those friends that Victor enjoyed spending a lot of time with at the university. Victor had shared the Gospel with John several times.

One of those days, he finally answered, saying,

"Oh, I get it now! So this Jesus, really, he is like a Buddha, right?"

With those kinds of statements from someone one has been evangelizing for quite a while, one can become quite discouraged – if not mightily – with the task a missionary strives to fulfill. You might think you must be in the wrong vocation, that you are wasting your time, and should completely change your vision. But things would soon start changing for Victor and Peggy. One day John came knocking on the Colombo-British front door. When Victor opened it, he saw he had quite an urgent demeanor. Despite that, Victor remembered John's words not too long ago about Jesus – comparing him to a Buddha – and wasn't really in the mood for chatting about faith with him anymore. But John was a good friend, who had come to the house time after time to visit, so Victor asked him to come in. What John said when he sat down took him by surprise.

"Victor, I have observed you – how you treat your wife; how much you love your son. I have never seen that before, but I think it's excellent. I want to be able to treat my own family in this way. How can I be like you? Can your Jesus help me?"

Each fruit – each person – who chooses to be a follower

of Jesus in China, especially under the communist regime, knew what he or she was getting into. They were willing to suffer persecution; they knew what awaited them in their walk with Jesus on this earth. Christianity is so much more than being part of a social club or an opportunity to make new friends on a Sunday morning and, from time to time, go to a BBQ. It's the state of obedience to the Lord, having received salvation as a gift from Jesus, and then being willing to lay down one's life completely, even to lose it completely, for the message of the Gospel. Sadly, despite the enormous underground church in China, the percentage of those who know Jesus is low compared to those who don't. It's an ideal place to invest your life serving the Lord amongst the unreached – those who have never had the opportunity to hear the Gospel or the name of Jesus.

"Ask me, and I will make the nations your inheritance, the ends of the earth your possession." – Psalm 2:8. Have you already asked the Lord for a nation or a few nations? Ask Him, then wait and listen, and He will speak to you.

Sit on Your Bibles

15

The missionaries used to get together to have times of prayer, intercession, praise, and worship as a family. They also encouraged each other on a regular basis, sharing testimonies, miracles, and present and future challenges. This was a recurring monthly event at an established time accorded by the team - and it was a priority for everyone. Being in a family and feeling the support of brothers in arms would help dissipate the attacks of the enemy, whose aim was to cause loneliness, frustration, discouragement, depression, and ultimately, for them to be ineffective or leave the mission field.

When we find ourselves isolated, it is easier to feel lonely. It's harder to fight - we get tired faster - but when we surround ourselves with people who love the Lord with all their heart - and, therefore, love us, things are better, for two are better than one.

On a particular night, Victor received a dream from God. This dream wasn't an answer to prayer - as most of them were. It wasn't a dream showing future blessings to come, such as the approximation of a new member of the family that would soon arrive. Instead, this was a dream of warning. In the progression of the dream, Victor saw how secret agents of the government, wearing black suits and glasses, broke into his home during one of the missionaries' meetings while they were in the middle of praise and worship. They proceeded to take them to prison, where they would be punished for crimes against the state, such as praising the Lord, a God other than the god of communism.

As soon as he woke up from his sleep, Victor contacted the other missionaries and told them about his dream that night. He told them to pray fervently and fast for God to stop that dream from coming true.

About two weeks after the warning, the Ywamers found themselves together in Victor and Peggy's apartment, praying and submerged in the presence of the Holy Spirit. They were in the middle of singing praises to God when multiple heavy knocks were suddenly heard at the front door, accompanied by a voice that demanded harshly in Chinese that the door be opened immediately. The missionaries became silent; some of them became pale; they knew that indeed some of them, if not all, could be incarcerated - or at least deported from the country, never able to return if their ultimate purpose for being in China was uncovered. Victor acted swiftly. He walked towards the door calmly, then turned around and spoke to the others in a whisper,

"Sit on top of your bibles, quickly! Keep on singing and playing the guitar."

Victor approached the door; the others tried to pretend as best as they could to look as calm as possible - and not as worried as they really were. Upon opening, Victor was looking eye to eye with the official supervisor of all foreigners residing at the university; he had an air of impatience and indignation around him. He was escorted by three government agents; dressed in black, just as Victor's dream had portrayed them.

"What are you doing here?" the official asked repeatedly in a very authoritarian tone as he and his men walked into the apartment. Their eyes scanned every corner of the residence.

As he entered the living room - where all the missionaries were, doing their best at acting calm. Victor looked at the office with a smile and said,

"We are just here having a good time together. We are singing songs from our own countries. So if you please, sit, and we can have some tea together."

As he realized that he was interrupting a friendly and harmless reunion of foreigners, the supervisor and his agents were totally embarrassed. And walking backward, hands clasped together, bowing their heads politely, they made it clear they didn't want to be a burden to the foreigners' hospitality. As soon as the door shut, there was a pause as all the missionaries processed mentally what had just happened. Then came forth the prayers of thanksgiving, laughter, and praise to the Lord for having warned them of what could have happened and for protecting them from a deeper search of the house, which would have ultimately exposed the Bibles they were sitting on, which would have been problematic, to say the least.

Nowadays, many missionaries are exposed and deported from China or simply cannot acquire a visa to stay after spending more than 5, 10, or even 20 years in the Eastern Giant. I invite you, my dear reader, to take some time to pray for these missionaries, for they have invested their lives in this country. The psychological, emotional, and spiritual wounds, burnouts or even traumas are a reality they must face upon leaving behind their loved ones, friends, disciples, and the land they loved so much, the land for which they had prayed so many years, even before they arrived there. Pray also for the local believers, for when they are found to be sharing about Jesus, they are not deported, but could end up in prison, or in extreme cases, disappear.

Stop the Fast

16

Amongst the missionaries residing in Chengdu, there was a couple that hailed from the United States. Jim and Sally had recently arrived in China to work hand in hand with the other Ywamers. All the local missionaries had great joy embracing the two new workers into their lives, for they were young and passionate, and Jim was also an exceptional piano player. He had quite the talent. He brought a new touch of heavenly inspiration and music to the times of praise and worship. The man had the gift of leading people through his voice and piano into deep worship in the presence of the Lord. Everyone enjoyed his talent and benefited from his heart of a worshipper.

Surprisingly, out of nowhere, Jim started to feel a strange pain in his body. He decided to go to the Chinese doctor, where he received some bluntly unexpected and devastating news. This particular doctor wasn't the kind of man to be concerned with the patient's emotional well-being. Hence, his declarations were straightforward and direct. He didn't try to soften the blow of the news in the case of it being bad news. This was one of those cases, unfortunately.

"Sir, you have cancer. It would be best for you to return to your country and enjoy the last couple of months you have left with your family and friends."

Just like Jim, the other missionaries were stunned upon hearing the dreadful news. A time of fasting was announced for all the Ywamers living in Chengdu. "If God brought him to

China, He can heal him too!" They all prayed fervently for their new friend; they spilled tears before the Lord, crying out for healing for Jim's body. After two days of this, they received their answer simultaneously from the Holy Spirit.

"Stop the fast; I have a special job for him here."

The response wasn't easy to accept for all, but they were convinced that the Lord had spoken clearly. With a sad farewell, the couple returned to Hong Kong to see a cancer specialist. They received the same answer from him – he had to go home to enjoy the last months of his life with his family and friends in the United States. And as if it was timed, after exactly two months, Jim passed away, to be in a much better place. Who knows what kind of extraordinary job the Lord had for him in the heavenly realms. Indeed he is there, fulfilling that task, surrounded by myriads of angels in a scenery that would be impossible to describe in a book like this with human words.

Tibet:
Rhythm Change

17

Victor continued studying the language as best as he could. However, it still remained a giant that taunted him. The words seemed to refuse to be correctly pronounced every time Victor opened his mouth. After only having been in Chengdu for three or four weeks, other foreigners from Korea, Europe, and the United States had already surpassed Victor's Mandarin, which he had been working on for over two and a half years - and Victor knew it better than anyone. One day in a meeting, another missionary approached Victor to speak with him. His approach was as if he were going to make some sort of proposal. He greeted Victor and reached into his pocket, where he retrieved a small piece of paper, which he quickly thrust into Victor's hand. Victor looked at the piece of paper and saw it had some writing on it, which he did not understand. The language was foreign but adapted to the Latin alphabet for easier reading.

"Try it, Victor. Read it, please." The young man asked him eagerly.

Victor proceeded to read the strange words out loud. As he read, his friend's face lit up with glee. His smile started to spread as Victor continued to read. Victor obviously did not understand what he was saying; "confusion" was written in capitals on his forehead.

"Why are you making me read these words, brother?" he finally asked.

"Wow, Victor!" he answered with great excitement; "you pronounce the Tibetan language perfectly!"

Victor's eyes lit up; Mandarin had been such a test of patience and endurance - sometimes a torture - for the previous two and a half years. "How could Tibetan be any easier?' he thought. It seemed almost impossible. This whole moment seemed very strange to him, and he kept it in his heart.

After a few weeks, just a few days from completing three years of living in Chengdu, Victor had another dream from the Lord. In this particular dream, Victor found himself in a small classroom. A few students were sitting at their respective small desks – they had been waiting for him. Victor walked over to the blackboard, which hung on the wall in the middle of the room. He started writing on the board with a piece of chalk in his fingers. What could be read, once Victor was finished writing, was "Everything that was in Jefferson's mouth was faith." Victor awoke from his sleep immediately, surprised and dwelling on the dream he had just had. Yes, he remembered the words that he himself wrote on the board - but more importantly, all the students were Tibetans! As the sun rose that morning, Victor shared the dream with Peggy. It was clear that the messages they had received from God lately pointed to Tibet. Peggy agreed to the possibility of them having some sort of future there.

Victor, because of the dream, also decided to do some research about Thomas Jefferson. Victor knew very little, if anything, about Jefferson. Still, every time he asked an American about the man, he learned less and less – and became more confused. Finally, what he managed to put together was that he was an author of the Declaration of Independence of the United States – a nation that had supposedly been founded on the Bible and on submission to God's law in its beginnings. Maybe the Lord wanted to see Tibet renewed with new foundations, Biblical ones, and that they declare their independence from idolatry and mysticism.

Some days later, with a day left until Victor's 40th birthday, he was on his knees praying to his heavenly Father at seven o'clock in the morning. While he prayed, a vision was suddenly laid out before his very eyes. It was like a large scroll literally being opened before him. In the vision, the image was of indescribable beautiful Asian scenery. There were three gigantic peaks in front of him - all covered in tons and tons of fresh white snow. Then, Victor saw a man far away, standing on one of the peaks. He wore a fine Tibetan robe with colored borders and a red scarf tied around his head. His cheeks were red, burnt by the sun and icy wind. The young man looked out from his vantage point. His deep eyes scanned from left to right the horizon, but without being able to find whatever it was he was looking for. His expression was that of hopelessness, as seen in a victim of war as she looks at the reporter's camera, as someone who has suddenly lost his home and wishes only to satisfy his hunger with a piece of bread. It was somewhat strange to see someone surrounded by such beautiful scenery yet unsatisfied, still searching for something more.

Victor woke up in a very thoughtful mood. Who was that young man? What was he looking for across the horizon? Victor knew the dream had a specific message for him, but he didn't know exactly what it was at the time since the Lord hadn't revealed it to him. But Victor didn't worry; he knew the Lord would connect the dots for him in due time. And effectively, the answer didn't delay. The following day was Victor's birthday, and many workers in the mission field came to his apartment to share a celebration time together. One of the women present brought a postcard to Victor and said:

"I'm sorry that I only brought you a postcard, but the Lord told me to give you a specific bible verse you need to hear; Happy Birthday!"

He took the postcard and turned it around; on the back of it, he saw the following verse written in ink:

> I lift up my eyes to the mountains –
> Where does my help come from?

These words had an immediate effect, for Victor realized that the Tibetan man he had seen in his dream was seeking that which only Jesus could offer him. Now he understood that his work was to go to Tibet. He shared the word with Peggy - this last confirmation. She smiled, and they soon packed some bags for an exploratory trip to Tibet. The other foreigners that were also receiving words from the Lord for Tibet started a period of fasting for the journey because Xining - the border city between the Tibetan region and the rest of China - was completely closed to foreigners. Finally, after four days of fasting, the news came that Xining had suddenly been opened to foreigners! - Thank you, God!

They started on their journey to Tibet, which would last about twenty-seven hours by train. Xining was a city where foreigners could now reside legally. The trip there was very comfortable. Inside the train, there were divisions between cubicles. Each cubicle had a set of four bunk beds of 4 levels where each person could rest comfortably. There were big glass windows, which didn't open in order to keep the warmth inside the cubicles. Yet, the constantly changing scenery could be thoroughly appreciated. Next to the bathroom was a tap of hot water that was always available for free for the passengers; it was used mainly for making tea or Chinese instant noodles - which little Oscar took an instant liking to, especially the spicy ones. The family had to increase their toilet paper budget. The whole trip was delightful, and time seemed to fly by. They were in Xining in no time.

When they arrived, they saw that Xining was quite a small city populated by Tibetans, Hui Muslims who were descendants of the Muslims from ancient eastern Europe and Russia, and the Han Chinese. The town was home to about 100,000 people, and the missionaries comprised almost all the foreign community. During the winter, the city would be covered entirely in white - no home would remain untouched by the snow. For many, it would be a challenge to even leave the front door of their buildings since it would be reinforced by almost a meter of snow. During the summer, the landscape would dramatically change. The parks in the city would come to life, colors would spring forth from thousands of flowers, and the relentless hot sun would come out from its hiding place and burn the remote city of Xining. During autumn, when summer dies and winter is on its way, the town would be covered in a cloud of dust brought forth by the wind currents hailing from the northern Gobi desert. Even today, people wear a mouth cover when they leave their homes to protect themselves from inhaling so much dust and excessive smoke.

Victor, Peggy, and the other missionaries had to convince the university's board of directors to allow them to study there. Only then did universities in Xining have the government's authorization to host foreigners. These would be the first. The missionaries had several meetings with the university directors and with government officials. Finally, the foreigners proposed a term fee of $600, higher than the Tibetan or Chinese would pay. With that, they were given their welcome by the officials. Nowadays, many foreigners, some of whom are missionaries and some of whom are simply wanting to study Buddhism or start a business, can study in Xining with much freedom, all thanks to God and to a few brave missionaries who ventured into this land believing that the Lord would open a door for them, relying on His guidance the whole time.

The return trip to Chengdu wasn't as pleasant as the coming – especially for Peggy and Oscar. A series of landslides had occurred between Chengdu and Xining, blocking some of the train tracks. All trains were canceled. Since traveling by train wasn't an option, the family decided to return by air. However, they discovered that all air tickets had already been sold out due to the sudden train cancellations. There wasn't even one left. So, a sole option for traveling remained: they'd go by bus.

The buses that went from state to state were usually in pretty bad condition, without mentioning the mountain roads, many of which were basically tracks of dust and sand, which, when caught up in the wind, would fill the buses through the many holes in the floor and the glassless windows. No one on the bus could escape the blanket of dust. The passengers resembled an excursion making its way out of the Sahara desert – after a sandstorm! Keeping little Oscar all covered up would present a challenge, yet soon, the dust affected him, and he began to cough. Peggy was alarmed, and they were all very uncomfortable, squeezed into the back of the bus.

The bus made a few stops at small restaurants and shops in towns along the way so that passengers could purchase snacks and drinks. One time Peggy got off the bus to buy noodles, but for some reason, was not even looked at by the waiter, perhaps not knowing what to do with foreign women. Even though he was first in the queue, someone else would be served, the bus would start, and Peggy and Victor, who'd come to help, had to leave foodless. As Victor watched his wife in frustrated tears and his son screaming even louder, he finally turned complainingly to God:

"Why do you want to take us to Tibet? Don't you see my wife and son are crying?" The Lord answered him with another question:

"Victor, I clearly see the suffering that Peggy and Oscar are going through. I know it's difficult for you. But here I ask you, are you still willing to follow me to Tibet?"

Victor asked his wife: "Peggy, do you still want to go to Tibet?"

With tear-filled and reddened eyes that momentarily connected with Victor's, she said:

"Yes, I still want to go to Tibet."

The tension in the atmosphere was broken. Calm and peace invaded. In no time, Victor, Peggy, and Oscar miraculously were promoted to better seats on the bus, and thus they soon fell asleep for the rest of the night.

Waking up the following day, Peggy found herself looking at a stunning landscape. Outside the window, she saw great white peaks covered in snow, which stood tall, blocking the horizon, imposing their authority over the green flatlands that fell under their sight. Along the misty morning plains, there were women dressed in thick skins milking the Yaks. The Yaks looked quite different from any other cow Peggy had ever seen. They had so much more hair – enough to make a few rugs – which protected them from the icy winds. They had a majestic air about them and looked powerful. Unlike other livestock, Yaks are adapted to live at more than 3000 meters high. Which is quite convenient since the general Tibetan altitude is about 4000 meters above sea level.

At its high altitudes, Tibet is composed of many large lakes; cold and desolate flatlands; and some of the planet's highest peaks – including Everest, which is shared with Nepal. One of the names by which Tibet is known is "The Roof of The World." And there it was, right in front of her very eyes. After three years in Chengdu – and a short visit to Xining – only God knew the adventures, tribulations, laughter, and tears that would await her and her family in this great and mysterious land.

Tibet is the center of mystic Buddhism on Earth. It's home to the priests of Buddhism, who some claim to be powerful handlers of mysterious supernatural forces. This would be the land for Victor, Peggy, and Oscar during the rest of their stay in China. Finally, they arrived at the land of the dream that Victor had seen. The ice-cold wind, the white peaks, and the Yaks on the meadows seemed to bid the family "Welcome," as if knowing they would soon return to settle.

After 35 hours on the bus, they eventually arrived back in Chengdu. The family immediately went to their university apartment. As they opened the door, little Oscar ran straight for Victor and Peggy's room, bounced up and down on their bed, enjoying the exhilarating freedom of movement, and flopped-fast asleep – exhausted from the long journey and glad to finally be able to sleep horizontally. For Peggy, it was a strange sensation to be back at home; only some hours ago, on that bus, she had had the unconscious feeling that the journey would last forever.

After returning to Chengdu, they knew they would only spend a little time there. Soon they would leave, along with a small team of missionaries, with their sights set on Xining – to live!

The group of missionaries consisted mainly of young families. Amongst them, there was a couple from Singapore. Lately, the Lord had blessed them extraordinarily – similar to how Victor and Peggy had been blessed about two years ago. They had welcomed a beautiful baby girl into their family. Her name was Lim Hui.

On a particular occasion, Victor and Peggy were in their Uni apartment. The regularity of the day was broken by hefty and desperate knocks on their front door. Something was going on outside their door, and it sounded frantic. Victor and Peggy hurriedly went to open the door together. It was the Singaporean couple – Lim Hui's parents. They were hysterical and with reason.

Lim Hui was dying.

Peggy immediately ran to the Hui apartment across the hallway. She found little Lim there, lying completely motionless. Her face had lost her natural pale color; it was blue. Peggy knew intuitively what she had to do. She bent over little Lim Hui's body, placed her own hands upon the girl, and simply said:

"Jesus, breathe your life into her."

Immediately Lim Hui's chest began to rise and fall. She recovered her breathing – and her life. The blue vanished from her face, replaced by her natural appearance. A miracle had just taken place. The Singaporean child had been rescued from the clutches of death itself. The doctors had been unable to do anything to save her; only God was able to. That day became a day of celebration for every single one of the missionaries in the city.

Up to today, the missionaries who were there during that time tell the story of the little girl God brought back to life, a little girl who now is a grown woman with an incredible account to tell.

The miracles we read about in the Bible, such as the healing of Peter's mother-in-law, the resurrection of the widow's son at Elijah's hands, and Jesus' own resurrection, are all historical accounts, the latter being supported and confirmed by many different witnesses. But the power behind those miracles is not confined to the pages or times of Biblical occurrences. It continues to be as real and powerful today. As sons and daughters of God, we have the authority to exercise divine healing and proclaim miracles through the Holy Spirit's power. "Did I not tell you that if you believe, you will see the glory of God?"

Two Nations at War

18

Although the Tibetan language was grammatically more challenging than Mandarin and had a completely different alphabet to Latin, it turned out to be much easier for Victor to pronounce – as for most South Americans. Victor was enjoying this phase of studies in Xining much more than the studies he had gone through in Chengdu. Mandarin had been a three-year-long desert for Victor to walk through.

Being one of the few foreigners, and the only Colombian at the university, Victor was swiftly chosen to be the coach of the two college football teams; one team of Tibetans, the other of mainly Chinese. Victor was naturally quite a good footballer, but being in Tibet, he was the best! In that era, football was tremendously lacking in presence amongst most Asian regions.

Once upon a time – while Victor was coaching his two football teams – a team of missionaries hailing from Australia arrived in the small city of Xining. They aimed to collaborate with and support the local long-term workers in Tibet. Plus, they also wanted the experience of evangelism amongst the unreached. The group leader eventually approached Victor with the intent of asking him to exercise his influence amongst the Tibetan footballers by gathering them together to speak with the Australians. The Aussies hoped to share their faith, and Victor agreed to help. The next step would be to talk with the Tibetans and determine whether they would be willing to gather with the foreigners. Once Victor presented the situation to his players, their captain responded:

"Namja" - the Tibetan name given to Victor, which meant Victorious - "we'd love to speak with them. We just have a question. Do they know how to speak the Tibetan language?"

The Aussies had learned the basics of Mandarin before setting out on their trip (as do most groups that come to China), and they could only communicate accordingly. But Amdo - the Tibetan language common to Xining - was entirely new for them. So upon hearing from Victor that the foreigners would only be able to converse in Mandarin, the Tibetan's answer was fast and without hesitation.

"Thank you, Namja, but if they know how to speak Mandarin and not Amdo, we are not interested in meeting them. But thanks anyway, Namja; we really like you because you speak our language. Many foreigners don't care to learn it."

Victor had heard quite a lot about the conflict between Tibetans and the Chinese government. The conquest of the Chinese over the Tibetan region had been a bloodbath; it had meant the loss of Tibetan sovereignty, some monasteries, loved ones, and their spiritual emperor, the Dalai Lama, who had fled to India and remains exiled up to this day. All this had left deep wounds in the souls of all Tibetans. Due to the occupation of their land by communist take-over, and the loss of many rights, every Tibetan longs for the day they will once again receive their freedom. Today many groups fight in the coliseum of diplomacy to make that freedom a reality. Others take extreme measures such as self-immolations (pouring gasoline on themselves and setting themselves on fire in public places) to show their defiance. This is a reality of our time. Since February 2009, more than 136 Tibetans have self-immolated - and probably many more by the time you read this.

Due to all this conflict, the Chinese government has exercised tighter control policies over the Tibetan region. There are very few cities where foreigners can reside for more than a week without a special and expensive permit. They will probably also be harassed by the police and coerced to move on. The cities where foreigners can live with a standard visa are on the borders of the Tibetan region, far from its heart and capital, Lhasa. In the past, some agencies of foreign intelligence, such as the CIA, were suspected of having secretly helped the Tibetans by giving them weapons training to resist the Chinese occupation. Therefore, the government views most foreigners in Tibet with a close watch. This means that foreign missionaries who wish to serve the hearts of Tibetans and Chinese in Tibet must tread with much caution, more than what is typically expected in other parts of China.

However, little by little, God has opened the doors for foreigners to study, open orphanages, and even start small businesses. Someday the government will understand that the Christian represents a Law-abiding citizen; that if given the liberty to live a life of integrity, a life of worship before the Lord, a life of proclaiming His name and Gospel, the Bible commands the sons of God to submit to the earthly authorities. The government would finally stop seeing Christians as a threat through their distorted lenses. The only ones who fear seeing the followers of Jesus as a threat are the powers of darkness – and all their puppets.

Victor realized soon enough that as he saluted a Tibetan in his own language, he would receive a very different reaction than if he greeted him in Mandarin –no matter how courteous he could be. Soon he was invited to many homes, firstly by his friends at college. They just wanted to talk, eat, and exchange culture between families. The worker who goes to Tibet would see the doors open much wider if they simply dedicate more time to learning the Tibetan language. Some have employed this method lately, giving much fruit to their friendships.

Despite this extra favor, Victor had to remain very discreet concerning how, when, and with whom he would share his faith. He had to first develop a solid and trust-based relationship with the individual, to prevent any leaks of information causing Victor, Peggy, and Oscar's stay in China to be in jeopardy. Therefore, today the worker who wishes to share his or her faith in China must be cautious, brave, smart, and most of all, Spirit-guided regarding communications in any direction. But the most crucial requirement remains this, and it will never change, to have an intentional daily prayer life that connects us to God, seeking His input, for He is our sender.

If the Holy Spirit has called you to go down in the well - missions - whether it is to a country governed by Buddhism, Hinduism, Islam, or secularism, don't worry so much about having the "keys" to being a "super-missionary"; focus more on developing a vibrant life of intentional prayer. The spirits of frustration, discouragement, and depression frequently made aggressive assaults on the Colombo-British family. Still, Peggy and Victor were firmly devoted to prayer - a characteristic that society seems to want to replace with the "casual" prayer pronounced internally when bored, before sleeping at night, or simply when there is nothing better to do. It could be compared to the physical body becoming stronger with small bites of sweets during free periods. That's crazy! The body needs nutritious food on a regular basis; how much more should the spirit be nurtured and in the presence of the God who is the author of and can protect and strengthen our faith? Even Jesus, the Son of God, ardently sought these times of solitude with His Father. Due to a lack of this intentional prayer life, we can hear every once in a while a sad story about Christian missionaries who went to some nation to be light and ended up embracing the darkness they initially thought to defeat.

Victor and Peggy were in China for a total of six years, three in Chengdu and three in Xining. They laughed joyfully and saw their work's fruit as people came to know Jesus for the first time. During that time, they also had two children, Oscar and a beautiful girl whom you'll meet in the following chapter. They were special guests on radio and television channels. They served in orphanages showing some of Jesus's love to children who had never experienced the love of a mother and/or father. They had been received as ambassadors with great honors, and they were, at times, in desperate conditions.

They cried and suffered; they had to stand firm when others falsely claimed that the will of God was that they return to England - threatening to diminish their financial support. Victor went to the schooling of humility during his numerous ups and downs - although it seemed that there were more downs than ups - while learning the local language, to be perfected as fire is perfected when put through the fire. They saw Chinese and Tibetans give their life to Jesus; these went on to become disciples that, in turn, led their own to know the

Lord. Victor and Peggy were friends with Jesus in a land where He had few friends. He continues to call faithful workers to visit this ancient land. And you know what? He might be calling you... have you asked him yet?

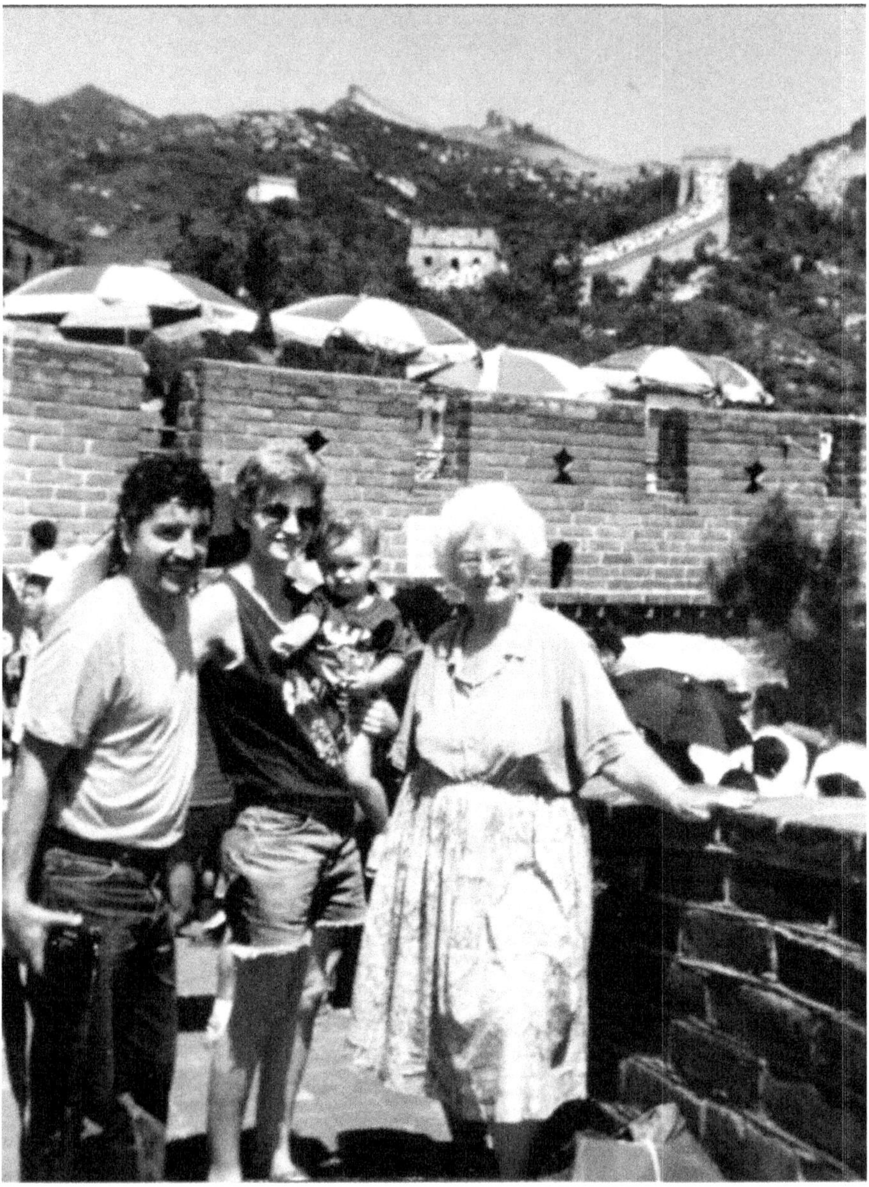

Pioneers' Suffering

19

In 1994, after five years of living in China – two of which had been lived in the remote city of Xining – Peggy was pregnant again with a beautiful little girl. Little Oscar was three years old now. Peggy was drawing close to the due date, and she remembered very well the conditions for giving birth to her son. She remembered the university hospital in Chengdu – and a feeling of lacking privacy. Conditions hadn't been the best for her. But now they were in Xining, and conditions were much worse in this relatively small, isolated town of China. The rooms were filthy, and the administration had low standards of hygiene and health regulations. As a result, Peggy didn't feel comfortable with the prospect of giving birth in Xining.

Peggy and Victor decided to set out on a trip to England, where the upcoming baby would have her great welcome into the outside world. This trip's benefit wasn't only limited to the conditions of the hospital; Peggy would also enjoy being surrounded by many loved ones for a few weeks. In addition, it would be an excellent opportunity for Victor and Peggy to relax and rest a while from the psychological tension of constant ministry and living in a country where said ministry could get them in trouble.

So they went to England, and the delivery was a success. At the age of 41, Peggy had no problems at all. They officially welcomed their little princess into their lives. Victor and Peggy named her Nathalie Vida. The root meaning for Nathalie in French refers to The Birth of Christ. The birth was healthy; she was surrounded by tranquillity and loving care. The only unusual thing was that the first night after giving birth, Peggy woke up in her ward to the deafening cries of a baby. The screams were coming from the incubation room. Peggy wondered what poor mother had a baby with such potent lungs and vocal cords.

Soon a nurse walked past Peggy's bed, so she asked her about the crying baby - it turns out Nathalie was the cause of all the noise! Peggy left her bed immediately, and with all her fatigue due to the delivery, she made her way to the incubation room. She saw Nathalie lying there and longed to have her beside her, so she brought wee little Nathalie to her bed to spend the night next to her mother. Despite those early screams, Nathalie brought great joy and happiness to the family; it was as if laughter and jokes were built into her DNA.

After a few months, the family readied themselves to return to China. There they would get back to hard work with Chinese and Tibetans, sharing their faith and the love of Christ. Once they arrived back at the mission field, Victor and Peggy started to perceive a threat to their work and stay. It was a subtle but gradually increasing coldness of their spirits. They felt more fatigued and tired than ever. It seemed harder and harder to seek the Lord and be refreshed in their spirit. This started to affect their relationships with other workers. They arrived at a point where they couldn't get along well with a certain couple that had recently been given a leadership position. Frustration and depression started to knock at the door, laying siege to the family. The situation as a whole became increasingly confusing. But, as it tended to occur during these moments of tribulation, they received a message from the Lord through dreams.

In this dream, Victor saw many missionaries who worked in Xining and across China. But it was a pretty sad picture; they were all leaving, never to return. Some left Tibet, and some left the organization as a whole. Upon waking up, Victor started to pray about what he had seen. In a few days, he shared this dream with the supervisor of the missionaries - but he didn't seem to give it any weight. As time went on, Victor and Peggy noticed that the same frustration, depression, and division that had been assailing them was taking place amongst the entire network of missionaries in China simultaneously. And in the end, many packed their bags to leave China – and the missions organization. The Pulidos decided to buy their tickets too. Once they did so, they held to a tradition most missionaries used to do in China when moving. They gave all their possessions to whatever other workers needed or wanted to have them. The only object that was sold was a guitar – which the buyer insisted on paying for. There was quite a farewell from the other Christians for the Colombian British family. They had wept together, laughed, held out against the biting cold, witnessed miracles together, and seen heavenly family depart to their home in God's arms. They were a true family, not perfect, but with deep and strong bonds. They would remain in touch for the many years that remained, wherever they would be.

Now, there was only one problem with this whole trip to the United Kingdom. Victor's UK visa had expired; they would have had to journey east to Beijing to renew it. Neither Victor nor Peggy intended to do that, so they prayed to the Lord to provide another solution. And that's precisely what happened. As if customary (this shouldn't surprise you anymore), Victor had a dream in which he arrived at Heathrow International Airport in England and eventually found himself sitting in a waiting room. In an adjacent room, there was a meeting going on between three men, nothing less than the top authorities of the airport immigration. The topic of the discussion was whether or not they would allow Victor entry into the UK. After a while, one of the three approached where Victor was sitting. Stretching out his hand, which contained Victor's passport, he said,

"Welcome to England."

The Lord had never lied to Victor, so the family left China towards England with a great sense of tranquillity, knowing God assured their entry.

As they stepped off the plane at Heathrow, they had to step in line to go through a customs check. Usually, someone without a valid visa to enter the country would be pale and sweating at this point, but Victor kept his calm. He completely trusted the Lord and that He'd fulfill His promise. Logically, as he passed through the checkpoint and the official saw that a certain stamp was not there, he sent him accompanied by guards to another room to be interrogated by some other migratory officials.

He explained his reasons for what he'd "failed" to do.

"It was too risky for us to go to Beijing. We're missionaries, and the police would have discovered our intentions if we had renewed the visa in China."

One must understand that in 1995 the bureaucracy epidemic had not quite reached its current heights in Western Europe. Victor simply explained to them that he needed to enter England despite not having a visa – since somebody had to provide for his English wife and children. Soon after this, as he had seen in the dream, the three top authorities of the airport were together in an adjacent room. They talked and discussed the situation for minutes, which seemed like hours. Once in a while, one of the men turned his head to observe Victor's behavior, both in himself and towards his family. Victor didn't know how to act naturally while under scrutiny. Peggy reminded him with low whispers,

"Keep calm, Victor. Play with your children."

After what seemed like an hour, one of the men came over to Victor.

"We want to help you, Victor, because you need to provide for your family. Can you prove that you haven't overstayed your visa time in the past? That would make it much easier for us to let you in."

That was easy; Victor had his old passport with him, which he handed over to the official,

"In there, you can find my old visa, and you will find that the stamps prove I left England nine months before the visa expired."

The official smiled with satisfaction.

"That's great! This makes things a whole lot easier."

In about an hour and a half, the man returned to the room where the family was waiting.

"Victor, you are the man of the house; you are a father and husband, and you must provide for your wife and children. Here's your visa. Welcome to the United Kingdom."

And so they entered Great Britain. They went straight to the city called Slough, where Peggy's mother was. Her church generously provided a home for them to live in for the time they'd be there, and quite conveniently, close by, there was a school for Oscar, who was already five. The house provided for them was a typical English house. It was a completely carpeted two-story house with a beautiful open space and garden behind it, partly surrounded by a wooden fence and a wall of pine trees. The neighborhood was constituted of families that were either Christian, Muslim, or

Hindu. And such was the metropolitan city of Slough. Soon they had many new friends in the neighborhood and in St. Paul's Anglican Church, which had supported them generously and constantly for years.

Victor and Peggy started looking for work as soon as they arrived. To everyone's surprise, Victor had also received a dream concerning this job hunt (surprised, right?). This dream actually had come to Victor while he was still in China, right before leaving. In this dream, he saw himself wearing a blue overall, and a yellow cap, as a worker for a dirty and greasy factory. Soon afterward, Victor was accepted to work at a large bakery where they made all kinds of mouthwatering cakes, muffins, and other delicious pastries that are great for diets. In addition, he was given the task of cleaning the floors.

It was a bit of a shock for Victor to do this because he had often told himself, "I'll never work for men again; only for the Lord." Sometimes the Lord uses such circumstances to deal with our inner pride to create discipline, and in certain circumstances, to benefit and bless others, such as the occasions when Paul made and sold tents. But Victor took it with gladness and joy, seeing it as an opportunity to be light amid much darkness. Most of his co-workers in the lower ranks of the industry were from Pakistan, Iran, and India - similarly cultured to that of the South American or at least slightly more than with an American or European. In addition to the natural flavor of being a Colombian, Victor had God's grace - for which Victor rapidly received some excellent news from his supervisor.

"Victor," the man said, "you always greet people when you come to work. You work well, and you don't talk negatively about us. But, on the other hand, the others tend to do their work mediocrely, insulting us and generally being lazy. So why are you like this?"

Victor answered, "Well, chief, I'm like this because I love Jesus and serve Him with all my heart. One of the two most important commandments is to love one's neighbor, and you all are my neighbors."

Victor was promoted to decorating, which meant putting the final cherry on each cake along the production line. It was undoubtedly a much better job than what he had before. After working there for a year, he was transferred to the catering section at Heathrow International Airport in London.

Victor and Peggy were out of Ywam for over a year and a half. They were spiritually dry and tired of missions – frustrated. Victor says today that he spent many days at a time without picking up his bible to read or pray. Whenever he attempted to, he would only read for a few minutes before getting distracted and uninterested.

When they started living in the UK, Ywam referred the family to a psychologist to process their war wounds. But he was too - how to say - professional – all intellect and no Spirit. They needed a renewal of their spirits, given to them by the Holy Spirit, which they couldn't obtain with the psychologist. They ended up slightly more frustrated than when they started the interview. Even the psychologist seemed like he urgently needed the help of the Spirit - more than they did. After a year and a half of living in Slough, working in factories, and attending St. Paul's church, the family visited a friend they had met in China. He ended up making a proposal to them.

"We are going to lead a Discipleship Training School focused towards China. Why don't you help us as staff?"

The couple explained to their friend their lack of desire to be involved with Ywam – and to be missionaries in general. Victor spoke quite frankly about his spiritual drought, his lack of biblical study, and his poor prayer life, to which the man exclaimed,

"That's exactly why God wants you to be with the team! He knows that if you were at a high level of spirituality, you would be full of pride and arrogance. Look at Jacob, who wrestled with God in his frustration and won. God left him with a limp but blessed him - that's how you are right now; God is with you in the battles and blessings."

Now, what the man had said made sense, taking into account the inner struggle Victor had with pride in Colombia and China.

"Victor, I understand that you are frustrated because I went through the same thing some time ago when my child was raped. You and those of your generation who were in China received the brunt of the war and battle for the soul of the Chinese. You were warriors in the first line of combat. You went through the pioneers' suffering."

Victor and Peggy decided to present this situation before the Lord in much prayer. The Holy Spirit talked to them soon after, confirming the truth that the North American had spoken to them.

"Those that go to China after you will not have to break through the land to enter it; you, Peggy, and your colleagues opened the gap. Others will come to sow the seeds and collect the harvest. But you were the prayer warriors; you desired spiritual warfare. I'm proud of you. You did it well, and I have new plans for you in England and Colombia."

The family understood that it was time to go to a different battlefield. They were refreshed in a big way during the DTS and then led a team on a short outreach of two months to Yunnan province in South China. Finally, after a season of being in England, Victor and Peggy received a message from the Lord to return to Colombia.

"Go back, Victor. You fulfilled your duty and your time in China. I'm grateful to you, son. Now you will train others in South America to go after the Eastern Giant."

Will I ever return to China?

20

Victor and Peggy happily returned to Colombia, for they would see Victor's mother, brothers, and sisters - along with all the friends they had made in Ywam before they left for China eight years before. They were also looking forward to the well-needed counseling their spirits needed. They were still in dire need of restoration. The only ones who were not so open to this significant change were Oscar and Nathalie, who were leaving behind all the friends, neighbors, school, and cousins they knew. But they soon seemed to adapt and get over it.

As they arrived in Bogota, the family lived with Victor's mother for some time, from whom they received much hospitality. They also enjoyed the calmness of the fields of the mountain range on the outskirts of Bogota - Anolaima. The couple didn't know for sure what part of Colombia, they would settle to grow their roots. Things weren't as they used to be before going out to China - much had changed since then. While Victor and Peggy were in Asia, the Ywam in Bogota -the only Ywam base in Colombia - closed down. Ywam lost the house they had, and some went back to their families. But it turned out this was all a clever strategy from the Lord for multiplication, which would change the future of Ywam in Colombia. The missionaries, who went home, were at first understandably disappointed and frustrated, confused and grieving – with many unanswered questions.

It was quite the grey season, painted with doubts and nostalgic feelings; it felt as if a whole battalion of soldiers in the heavenly armies had suddenly been disbanded after so many years of service and warfare. It was hard to break the bonds of fellowship that knit them all so closely together. Some of them didn't feel a sense of purpose anymore – others were clueless about what they were supposed to do now. Adapting to a "normal" life with "normal" jobs would be an arduous process.

Surprisingly, and quite unexpectedly, one by one, certain people started receiving words from the Lord to open new Ywam bases in other cities across Colombia. Each person or couple had made the journey to the city the Lord had put on their heart. From Bogota, young missionaries went to Medellin, Cali, Leticia, Cartagena, Ibague, and Bucaramanga. They planted themselves there to be used by God, multiplying disciples. The Lord apparently decided to use a similar strategy to that He used with the Tower of Babel - destroying the center of command of the missions organization, where everyone was quite comfortable - spreading the people to corners of the country, and building new centers where missionary work would be carried out, and thousands more would be trained and disciplined. So, now Victor and Peggy had many more options for where to go and settle.

Victor and Peggy had a wonderful meeting with Ricardo and Marilu Rodriguez, the directors of Ywam in Colombia. The latter were now setting up a base in Bucaramanga; Victor and Peggy felt led by the Spirit to join them. Their job seemed clear: to challenge, equip, and set young Christians on a path to serve the Lord in the Eastern Giant – China. When they arrived in Bucaramanga, they were heartily welcomed by the small group of Ywamers. Oscar and Nathalie were very soon involved in the children, and youth ministry called King's Kids, where they would learn to know God in a much more personal manner and make Him known to others through the arts and evangelism. Meanwhile, their parents would be working with the DTS. The doors opened for them to work with churches by teaching and sharing about Missions, walking in faith, and their experiences all over the world. Some of the topics for which Victor began to be invited to many places to teach were Spiritual Warfare and Hearing the Voice of the Lord.

At that time, they both had the chance to encourage many people to walk in obedience to Jesus, fulfilling the commandment given called the Great Commission. So Peggy started to run English schools, each lasting three months, intending to train and equip people for the ministry. A great variety of Christians came to these schools; it was a melting pot of denominations – from the most strict to the most liberal, from those who wore a suit and tie to sleep, to those who put on display the brand of their underpants and changed their hair color to bright green. Many began their genuine relationship with the Lord amid their English learning, switching from religion to relationship.

After a year in Bucaramanga, Victor was starting to feel restless, bugged by the desire to intensely take up once again his task and passion of sharing the Gospel to the unreached corners of the earth. Victor wasn't the only one aware of this growing restlessness, so the Lord gave him a dream – a strange one. When he closed his eyes at night and finally drifted off to sleep, he found himself standing at a bus stop with no bus. He knew he was awaiting the bus with the particular name "On the way to Tibet ."Victor stood at the station anxiously waiting, but nothing came. There was no sign of any incoming transport. Victor looked from left to right, examining the empty road, which remained desolate for what seemed at least two hours.

While waiting, Victor's attention got diverted to a small shop on the opposite side of the road. It was a small travel agency, and since the bus took its precious time to arrive, Victor decided to investigate the little shop. As he entered, he saw a young lady at the counter. Victor asked her for a map. She looked on some counters and retrieved a rolled-up map, which she laid out in front of him, and laying her index finger on a specific point on the map, she said,

"Guambia is here."

Instantly, Victor saw himself transported to a completely different sight. He was high up in the green mountains, and as he looked to his right, he saw himself accompanied by a man of low stature with long black hair. The man walked with Victor around the mountain and pleaded with him:

"Please come to teach us, brother Victor. Speak to us about Jesus."

"But you have many preachers whom you could invite to share, right?" Victor replied.

The man's features showed his sorrow as he answered. "We've already invited them, Victor, but no one wants to come. You come, we will host you and bless you, but we need to hear the Gospel urgently."

And with that, Victor woke up.

"What part of Asia is Guambia located in?... Maybe it's in Africa instead..." - Victor asked himself and God these questions for the next few days. Sometime later, Victor was doing some errands and paying bills in the city center of Bucaramanga. As he crossed a street, he found himself standing in front of a travel agency. He immediately remembered what he had seen in his recent dream; obviously, he had to check it out. No sooner than he had walked in, his eyes were anchored on a word, which was in the middle of an ethnic group map of the tribes in Colombia. The word was GUAMBIA. He hastily took the map and paid for it. Then, he rushed home as fast as he could. When he arrived, he excitedly showed Peggy the map where Guambia was displayed.

"It's here in Colombia! Close to Cali."

Peggy was excited to hear about this since she knew about the dream Victor had had a few weeks ago. The thing was, she really wanted to go with him, but the risk would be too great since the armed guerrilla groups dominated the whole area where the Guambianos lived. Taking an obviously foreign-looking woman there wouldn't have been wise. After praying about it, they both decided it would be better for Victor to go alone.

Victor made contact with the Ywam workers in Cali. Apparently, they had already had some evangelistic interaction with the Guambianos beforehand - but nothing to a great scale yet. When Victor called them, it turned out there were two young men who wanted to go very soon to Silvia - the capital city for the Guambianos - with the aim of carrying out an evangelistic campaign. Together with Victor, they came to an agreement in which they would take care of the dramas and theatre, and Victor would be the one to give the message of the Gospel at the end. Victor was eager to go and glad to be involved in the work that burned in his heart: to bring Jesus to the lost.

Upon arrival in Silvia, Victor understood the reason for not bringing his wife. On the main road which took them to the city, there were many military checks – only they weren't the government's military, they were the guerrillas – in which they took possession of cars, trucks, and motorbikes by force whenever it took their fancy. It was common to see children of sixteen or seventeen years old all dressed up in guerrilla uniforms, driving around in luxurious cars, which only the very rich of that time could afford to buy. For the first time, Victor saw women being part of these guerrilla groups. They wore dark glasses and camouflage, and with their college or university studies, they lectured new female recruits on their "revolutionary" philosophy. Who knows what Peggy's fate could have been if they had both insisted on bringing her.

As they arrived, they went straight to the school, where they would hold the campaign. They met the school's director – the woman of peace who opened the doors for them in town. This woman actually personally knew the local guerrilla leaders. When she asked them if they would give permission for the evangelistic campaign, they welcomed it... with only one condition, that they wouldn't speak anything against the guerrilla group or their "ideals ."Other than that, they were welcome to talk all they liked about Jesus.

That afternoon the group of Christians went all over the town, giving out invitations for people to come to the campaign. Every night, for the duration of that week, the school building was packed – more people came every night, and many gave their lives to the Lord. Victor's heart smiled as he witnessed what God was doing in Guambia, and even though he wasn't in Tibet, he was still grateful for being placed once again on the battlefield for peoples' souls. That didn't turn out to be Victor's only or last visit to the Gambian people; during the next two years, he went twice more, recruiting other Ywamers to go with him in the process.

On his last visit to the Guambiano believers, he was invited to preach in a new congregation high up on the mountaintops. While preparing his sermon, Victor prayed for the church and asked the Lord for a revelation about what He wanted him to preach about. The Lord gave him a vision about the congregation in question. In this vision, he saw a great caldron full of water set over a fire. The fire had heated up the water, which boiled and bubbled violently. The caldron had a metal plate that ran all the way through its center, dividing the water into two sections. The water was in full motion, but it was divided. Victor understood; the church in Guambia was divided.

As he shared this vision with the church elders, they knew immediately what he was talking about. Everyone in the church was passionately hungry and thirsty for more of Jesus, the Gospel, evangelism, and worshipping the Lord, but they were divided smack down the middle. Half of the church was against the planting of coca and marihuana on their mountains; the other half was in favor of it since, for many, it represented their only means of income – how would they provide for their families if they stopped?

Sadly, this was and continues to be a reality in some of the towns and small cities in Colombia and other parts of the world. The guerrilla groups prey on and harass the farmers and peasants when they are weak and in need. First, they show them how cereals and corn, amongst other crops, aren't producing much of a harvest. Then they point them to an easy solution: to sow cannabis and coca. For this, they are offered better rates and the assurance that the farmers won't have to worry about the distribution in any way; the guerrilla even provides their services in reaping the harvest themselves if that's what it takes to make the "yes" easier for the peasant. And, of course, desperate for a better income, many will agree to these propositions knowing that the chances of the Army coming through their area is minimum.

This was the last time Victor visited Guambia, partly because during the hike up the mountain to reach the church, his knees began to suffer and cause him considerable pain. The cartilage was getting damaged, and from then on, he had to be much more careful, for any kind of effort without warming up or cooling down properly would leave a constant ache in his knees for the next few days. During these years of visiting the Guambianos, Victor's thoughts turned to the glorious past – to all those precious years of mission work in China and the Tibetan Region. It was inevitable that nostalgic questions would surface in his heart, which knocked on God's door:

"Will I ever return to China?"

God's answer was as wise as ever. "Son, there are other nations on earth that I love in addition to China, and I want you to bless them while you train other young men and women to go to China. They will be able to do more than you could."

Cancer

21

It was late 2001, and Victor, Peggy, Oscar, and Nathalie had already undergone several trials. Peggy had succumbed to various episodes of very difficult vomiting and diarrhea. They were so strong that when Victor once came to visit her while she lay in bed after a particularly strong attack, Peggy looked at him with a lost expression, and in complete surprise, she exclaimed:
"Who are you?"
Peggy had lost her memory due to a minor brain hemorrhage. Victor's mother – Doña Blanca – was visiting at that time. Along with Oscar and Nathalie, she went into the room where Peggy rested; they were welcomed with the same surprising question and lost expression. Peggy's surprise grew increasingly on her face as she heard (as if for the first time) that she had a husband and two children and that it would be Christmas day in only a couple of days. Although her memory didn't return for a full day, she did her best to talk with her family in the most natural way possible – she had lost her memory, not her kindness and love. Oscar and Nathalie were most curious (and slightly scared) about this whole ordeal. They constantly tried to think of a fantastic event that had happened or was going to happen and would tell their mother about it to see who could surprise her most. Victor took her to the clinic, and after a couple of hours and a lot of rest, her memory started returning.

Peggy can remember being very sick, but even today, fourteen years later, she remembers nothing that happened during those two days.

Some time passed since the event when Peggy started feeling something uncomfortable in her side under her arm. She placed her hand under her side only to become pale and alarmed. Peggy immediately left for the hospital, fearing that the doctors might confirm her suspicions. Once in the medical practice, the doctor put her hand on Peggy's left side for a quick diagnosis. The doctor's expression changed from that of concentration to worry. Trying not to cause a panic, she said as calmly as it was possible for her:

"Señora Peggy, I'm sorry to inform you that you have a lump in your breast. It's as big as a golf ball. We'll take an X-ray to examine it further and find out if there's anything we can do if it's not too late. You'll have your results in a week's time."

Peggy's horror had just been confirmed. She remembered her own father, who had fought until his last breath in an unrelenting battle against cancer. And it had been an excruciatingly painful death indeed.

"Am I going to die? Will it be painful? How will I tell Victor? Will Oscar and Nathalie understand? Will they have to grow up without a mother and suffer my loss?" So many questions were running around in Peggy's soul, stealing her peace.

It was a challenge to see any light on the horizon; it was a tangibly dark period for Peggy. Victor felt his heart sink as he heard the bad news. He knew the possibility of treatment for his wife would at least be long and painful, as much for her as for the rest of the family. No doubt, he raised some questions to God. After all these years of service, why would God allow this illness to come upon Peggy? They both agreed to not tell Oscar or Nathalie for a while until they knew they had to.

They both decided to do the only thing they could in such a great crisis: Pray and Fast. With hands joined and bent knees, they raised their voice to the heavens, trying to trust as much as possible but with an undeniable passion and desperation. Victor prayed:

"Lord Jesus, thank you for your company and friendship with us. Thank you for bringing us up to this point. We ask in Your Holy name to heal Peggy. Take away the cancer and all ill. We rebuke the enemy and order him to flee. Thank you, Lord, for your love towards Peggy. Thank you because you are going to heal her. Amen."

They raised their voices that whole week with cries, tears, and pleading. If there was anyone who could heal Peggy, it was the God who loved them, called them, provided for their every need, and took them to China and back to Colombia. During that week, they didn't tell Oscar or Nathalie what was happening. Maybe they were too small to understand that the tension and the silence that seemed to have crept into their home were a symptom of the threat that loomed over Peggy's life. Despite the prayers, that week was an emotional roller-coaster for the couple. The horror of what might lay in store grew with every night and its nightmares.

When that feared day finally arrived, Victor and Peggy knelt by their bed one more time. They prayed. The room had a serious and tense atmosphere as they got ready to head out to the hospital. Those twenty minutes in the taxi were more nerve-wracking for them than all the cold and dusty bus rides on the Tibetan plateau.

They finally arrived at the clinic. After they'd waited for some time, the nurse finally brought out the respective X-ray results. Neither of them really even wanted to look. But when they did, to their surprise, everything seemed perfectly normal. There wasn't any visible tumor or lump... But they knew they weren't doctors. However, the nurse was intrigued and surprised, so she left at once to find the doctor, whose surprised expression was priceless.

"I... I don't understand, Señora Peggy", she said clumsily, tripping over her own words, "the test shows that there's nothing on your side. That's impossible! Let's check again." She put her hand once more on Peggy's side; her face remained a picture of utter wonder. "It's gone! It was here a few days ago, but it's gone now! I don't understand how this could have happened, Señora Peggy."

"I understand," Peggy answered with tear-filled eyes and a smile from ear to ear, "God has heard our prayers!"

Victor and Peggy didn't know how to express what they were feeling in totality. They hugged and didn't cease to thank God for the entire ride home. At last, they decided to tell Oscar and Nathalie. They were worried at first, and rightly since it all came as quite a shock. However, they also gave God the glory once they digested the entire picture. They were deeply enriched by experiencing the Lord's healing power in their own family. This had a more profound effect than any seminary ever could, and they wouldn't forget it for the rest of their lives.

After this event passed, Victor's best friend, the prophet Cristo Manuel (you might remember he was in Peru with Victor) visited them. He told Peggy she would never again lose her memory or have breast cancer. The Lord removed all traces of the disease. God's healing of Peggy was total and continues to be as such up to this day.

As it can happen in many Christian and missionary circles in the West, we can begin to see the incredible breakthroughs of God's power through finances, the birth of missionary societies, and even prophecy, and little by little, we can put the promises of healing power aside. We can get caught up in our different techniques of problem-solving and administration (which aren't bad) and start to forget that the most effective and practical tool to move a mountain is nothing other than true prayer. It's much more than a spiritual tradition. Be bold and take steps in believing that the Lord is concerned with much more than just your wallet. He can and will bring healing for you because Jesus took away those diseases on the cross. Remember, the supernatural is God's playground.

No Weapon...

22

The family spent six years in Colombia, 1997-2003, working with churches, encouraging other Christians to hear the Lord's voice and follow Him in obedience, and empowering many to take the Gospel to the unreached. They were overjoyed to see their children growing in the Lord and ministry. But the skies were gradually darkening, preparing to welcome the rise of a storm in Victor and Peggy's expectations. An old enemy they had encountered in China started to lurk in the shadows: Frustration and Discouragement. After six years of returning to Colombia, not a single person had stood up to the challenge of planting their life, some years, or at least some time, to bring the message of salvation to the Chinese and Tibetans. If it wasn't too evident on the outside, this frustration was certainly growing once again in the hearts of the two pioneers. They had no clue what the Lord had in mind for them in the coming months.

During one of the School for English in missions, the students and their director – Peggy – went to do the practical phase of the course in the Caribbean Islands called Trinidad and Tobago. They soon discovered that this country comprised people of many different cultures and ethnic groups. Approximately half of the population were Afro-descendants; the other half were Indian descendants, and a small minority with ancestors of North American, French, Spanish, British, or Arabic descent. Due to such a diverse inheritance, the names of the streets, neighborhoods, towns, and cities were named in various languages.

The group also found multiple religions all across the Island of Trinidad. There were Atheists, Hindus, Muslims, Christians, and witches.

The team had many opportunities to do evangelism in local schools and collaborate in some churches – all in English. They remained there for two months, supporting the local and young Ywam base, practicing their English at every chance. This task wasn't easy, considering that it came across to foreigners like a totally alien language when it was spoken with the local accent.

On returning to Bucaramanga, Colombia, someone very special to the family visited once again. If you're thinking of Cristo Manuel – Victor's lifelong friend who brought him a message when he wanted to rebelliously leave Ywam and who eventually followed the newlywed couple Victor and Peggy on the plane to their honeymoon – you guessed correctly. This time he arrived with a direct message from the Lord.

"You will all soon go to Trinidad and Tobago."

At first, Victor and Peggy didn't think much of this message, for the thought of going to live there had never crossed their minds; and they didn't see any motive for which they would be invited to move there. They thought they'd be in Colombia for many more years, continuing in the task they had of training and equipping young Latin Americans to go to China. It must have come as quite a surprise when some months later - after having heard the prophecy from Cristo Manuel - they received an email from Kevin – the director of the Ywam base in Trinidad. The message simply stated,

"I want to invite you to come to Trinidad. You can pioneer and lead the Discipleship Training School. If you accept, you can live in a house we are just about to finish building on our campus. You can live there until the Lord directs you to change location. What do you say?"

Victor and Peggy were a bit startled at the sudden offer, but they remembered the prophet's words. So they immediately set the task of praying about the proposal. Soon they packed their bags and made all the necessary arrangements to go to Trinidad and Tobago.

Once again, the move (the sixth one for the family) was challenging for everyone. There were very long farewells amongst Nathalie and Oscar's friends from the different ministries and workers of Ywam and, obviously, their dear pets, which had spent quite some years with them. But they knew that they were being obedient to the Lord, and therefore they prepared to leave with much joy.

Through many miracles, the Lord paved the road for the family to reach the Island of Trinidad - the major one being thanks to the loss and theft of one of their bags, which contained Oscar and Nathalie's Colombian passports, not to mention a camera and cash. This happened the same afternoon they were meant to take the bus to Cucuta, on the

Colombian border with Venezuela, where they would cross the border to catch the plane to Caracas and on to their destination. But, unfortunately, they left their bag in the taxi, which after being paid, drove off, never to be seen again. So, early the following day, they caught another taxi to the city center. When they finally found the government building in charge of the passport issue, they found the whole event to be quite tense, and with good reason, since the average waiting time to get new passports was two weeks. And they had to catch the Cucuta bus that afternoon.

They had been praying the whole taxi ride, asking the Lord to provide them with the right person to show them favor – without a bribe! It would be nothing short of a miracle if they received their new passports in time. So many people were standing in the queue when they arrived. Everyone was hoping to get some sort of legal document expedited or renewed. The place was relatively small and cramped, like a sheep pen. It was pretty hot since it only had two fans hanging from the ceiling, going around as slowly as the queues were advancing.

Victor and Peggy ignored the lines and went directly to one of the windows. They hurriedly explained the urgency of the case they found themselves in to the official. The guy behind the glass looked at them with a smile and said,

"Don't worry, sir and ma'am. I'm going to help you. Just fill out the following form," he said, handing them a form for each family member, "go to the bank to pay the appropriate fee, and immediately return here to pick up your passports."

Oscar and Nathalie had new passports given to them in only two hours – without a single bribe! That afternoon they were eventually sitting on the bus to Cucuta and soon in a plane crossing the sea to Trinidad and Tobago.

The real shock of changing homes wasn't only due to the trip. When they arrived at the airport, they were greeted with a wave of very humid heat, even though the day was already getting dark. Kevin and one of his four children eventually found them and greeted them with broad smiles on their faces. Soon the Colombo-British family was packed into their hosts' minivan. Once they had driven for about forty-five minutes, they reached a point where the road turned from asphalt to dirt and sand. Instead of driving past KFCs - which can be found on most corners of Trinidadian neighborhoods - they became submerged between two thick walls of high grass and enormous trees from which many vines hung as if expecting Tarzan to visit. It was completely dark when they reached their new home. They realized the entire mission's base was surrounded by a thick jungle, from which many strange lights and completely unfamiliar sounds came to them.

"Looks like we just arrived in some African jungle" - they all thought.

That first night was particularly tough for Nathalie and Oscar, who had never before lived in such a jungle-ish setting. So the entire family decided to spend that night huddled in Victor and Peggy's room. Once the lights were off, they could see the light bugs, which curiously flew over them, revealing their sporadic sparks. They heard the squawks and rustling of grass and bush coming from a few meters away from the house, where the jungle lurked.

"Do they bite? Are they poisonous? Could crocodiles or snakes be hiding under the bed? What about tarantulas? Surely they must have been watching us since we entered the house, waiting for us to fall asleep and attack!" dramatic thoughts, but quite true. These were some products of the children's imagination during those first couple of nights.

In a few months, they were used to their conditions. Oscar even invited one of his friends to come to sleep over for a weekend, with the condition that he bring his curious pet with him. Yes, you guessed it - if what you were thinking of was a fully-grown python. Nathalie adapted even better. She nonchalantly played with little and giant tarantulas they found hiding in the corners of the roofing - or behind curtains.

The Ywam base was situated on a 72-acre-sized piece of land in the deep jungle. There were small creeks that flowed close by the houses. The water level would rise and come up to the edges of the doors during the rainy season - which brought some unexpected guests from time to time. More than once, the Ywamers ate from the fruit of these guests: Cayman meat. If someone walked along the dirt road away from the base for about ten minutes, they would find an opening in the dense jungle. The children didn't take long to discover there was a creek at the end of the short trail, which expanded and deepened enough for it to be a pretty decent murky natural swimming pool. Soon enough, another missionary, the kids, along with Kevin and Sue's (Kevin's wife) children, had hung up vines from the thick tree overlooking the pool. They would compete to see who could swing off a tree on the bank of the creek with a vine making it far enough to get a hold of another vine halfway across the pool.

But the creek also had another guest. On one occasion, a pastor came to visit the missionary base. Victor was in charge of giving him a tour of the place. When they neared the end of the tour, they came to the jungle pool. As they walked through the trail and approached the water, something made Victor stop dead in his tracks. A crocodile, at least two meters long, crawled calmly along the opposite creek bank. Sensing the human presence, it looked straight at them and dove into the water. They didn't see it resurface. The chill of realizing they had other visitors to their hidden paradise dissuaded any swimmers for about two weeks from visiting the water. But soon, they were back in the water, enjoying the pool with the other missionary kids. They lost their fear of the jungle, its strange insects, and the large mammals which lurked in the dark. At one point, Oscar even went with Jason - Kevin's second oldest son - into the jungle after dark to try and purposefully find a crocodile with the hope of capturing it. Victor and Peggy led the DTSs for three years. They took missionary teams of young people to Nigeria, Tanzania, Suriname, and India, amongst other countries. Victor shared about Jesus amongst the Masai tribes of Africa, had close and dangerous encounters with lions, served India's "Untouchables," and equipped many to fulfill the Great Commission in whatever way the Lord had reserved for them.

Besides discipleship and training through the missions schools, the leader's vision also included building a great retreat camp for young people. There would be obstacle courses and various programs for the youth to experience fun, adrenaline, and teamwork, focusing on teaching about Jesus and giving the participants an environment to open up to Him. Unfortunately, this was a project of a high financial cost, and the progress was relatively slow most of the time, also thanks to the slow processing of legal matters in a government that was doubtlessly crippled by corruption.

One day one of Kevin's financial supporters donated a Toyota Prado, which was to be sold for a reasonable amount (in Trinidad and Tobago, cars were and continue to be extremely expensive), and the money was put towards the ongoing building of the obstacle courses in the camp. The plan had initially been to sell the Toyota as soon as possible since such a nice car would undoubtedly draw attention from greedy eyes in the rural area the base was located in. But it wasn't sold fast enough; instead, it was used occasionally to go back and forth from church on Sundays - amongst other things.

That fated week, Victor had been praying as he used to. He would walk off into the jungle and find his praying spots, usually on a hill beside a conglomeration of bamboo growths. Two dogs from the base usually escorted him, and he would stay there praying for hours. While praying that week, he felt the Lord give him a strong impression through a Biblical verse found in Isaiah 54:17, which says,

"No weapon forged against you will prevail...."

This didn't make much sense to Victor. Was the Lord talking about spiritual weapons in this case? Would he be tempted? In only four days, he would find out.

Next Sunday came around. Victor and his family weren't at church in the morning since they had guard duty for the weekend; instead, they would go to an evening service once everyone returned. During the morning, Oscar had been hanging around with a friend of his – a young American missionary called Mark. The rest of the family was inside the house; Peggy was reading a book, and Nathalie was showering. At about 4pm, Oscar and Mark were outside the tool shed, which was located on a hill between the residential houses and the classroom – about eighty meters from Victor's house. Oscar and Mark were sharpening some machetes and cleaning various other tools. The morning had turned into a beautiful afternoon. The birds were singing; the grasshoppers were chirping and jumping across the well-cut grass, and the sun shone on the land bringing out the intense green of the jungle as it habitually did.

In the distance, Mark and Oscar could hear the Prado approaching. Soon it emerged over the hill as it passed through the main gate, filled with Kevin's family. As it cruised through the base along the sandy road, it stopped halfway to their house; Kevin's youngest son got out of the car, closed the gate, and the car kept going. The boy joined Mark and Oscar in their work; he was always very curious. The three didn't even glance back at the car as Kevin drove it behind his house to park it, and that's when the screaming began.

Mark ran towards the right side of the house while Oscar went to the left – both armed with freshly sharpened machetes. As he jumped onto the sand road, Oscar was at the angle where he could see Kevin, the Prado, and the five masked men carrying hand revolvers and shotguns aimed at Kevin and the car. One of them saw Oscar and immediately lifted his gun, aiming straight at him. Oscar didn't wait around to see what kind of a shot the masked man was. In a fraction of a second, he had jumped off the left side of the road and was sliding and running down the sharp slope about ten meters from his house. He heard the man shoot twice at him, but without success. He ran to inform his family of the source of the screaming and gunshots they were hearing. As he looked for Peggy and Nathalie, he didn't realize that Victor had left the house to investigate and was now face-to-face with one of the masked criminals. (If none of this sounds familiar, please go back and read the introduction)

The man aimed his revolver at Victor – specifically at his head – who was accompanied by one of the dogs called Sammy. Victor and the criminal started their shouting exchange, Victor rebuking him and the other threatening to shoot him immediately. Sammy barked violently. Upon hearing the warning from the Holy Spirit to shut up, Victor obeyed. Still, he could feel the aim of the barrel readily focused on his temple. In less than a second, the man pulled the trigger.

"No weapon forged against you will prevail...."

The words of Isaiah resounded with the high-pitched whistle resulting due to the shot fired at such close proximity. As he looked at himself, he realized he wasn't dead; he was actually still standing. The criminal was now walking in the opposite direction, back towards the car, which was the object and reason for the attack. Victor hadn't been shot, for the masked criminal had moved his revolver out of Victor's direction and, for some reason, towards Sammy – who by that time was about eighty meters away, shaking as he hid under Peggy's dining room table; he was lucky to be alive.

Where had Victor received this courage? The bravery to stand up to the criminal holding a firearm aimed at his head at fewer than three meters, and instead of surrendering or backing away, he instead decided to command him to leave his territory. Where does that come from? The natural world has no explanation for this. But, the answer can become quite evident when God is put into the equation. His courage came from the Lord in the form of holy anger.

In the meantime, Kevin, who was now retreating from the whole commotion, had a constant squirt of blood coming out from the lower side of his neck, which he was applying pressure to with his left hand. He was losing a lot of blood and was beginning to stagger. Finally, Oscar came to help carry him down to Peggy's pick-up truck. He told his stunned mother to get the keys and turn them on so they could take Kevin to the hospital. Hopefully, the sound of growling engines would give the criminals the impression that many more people were in the base than they had initially thought.

"No weapon forged against you will prevail...."

Isaiah's phrase resounded in Victor's heart and mind. His heart was beating heavily. The Lord had once again sent him a message about the attack to come.

"Why didn't he kill me, Lord? He had the gun to my head!" But the Holy Spirit just answered,

"It's not your time yet, Victor. You still have many years ahead of you, upon this earth, with your family."

The man who had Mark pinned down had already lost interest. Mark saw his chance, so he got up and sprinted away from the scene, intent on finding a place to call the police. Some of the other Ywamers were coming out of their houses armed with whatever they could find; machetes, pic-axes, and hatchets. These were coming up behind Peggy, who was driving the pick-up, straight towards the Prado where Sue and her daughter had been locked in. The assailants didn't seem to want to risk an open confrontation. By this time, they had retreated into the cover of the jungle line without their prize: the Prado. They only managed to get away with about a hundred dollars in cash and an ancient cell phone.

Now, Sue was bleeding heavily from her hip; she had taken a bullet aimed at breaking the door lock since the assailants couldn't force the car open. The shot went through the door and into her hip. Those not in Peggy's pick-up helped Sue into the back seat; the rest jumped onto the rear cargo bed. As she saw the assailants had left for good, Peggy put all her strength on the accelerator and headed for the hospital. Usually, a drive to the hospital would take at least an hour and a half - Peggy made it in thirty minutes. With a policewoman sitting beside her, she drove as she'd never driven before, weaving in and out of traffic and accelerating like a Formula 1 racer. If a car refused to get out of her way, all the honking and the shouting from the kids in the back of the truck soon did the job. Upon arrival, Kevin and Sue were immediately taken to A&E. The others sat in the waiting room. They eventually heard Kevin's moaning in anguish as the doctors rapidly did everything they could to stop the bleeding.

The doctors said it was a miracle that both of them had survived or even that they could have continued living a "normal" life. The bullet had gone through Kevin's neck and shoulder without touching any major blood vessels or causing significant damage to the nervous system. After Sue was operated on and the surgeons successfully retrieved the bullet from her hip, they warned them that they wouldn't have taken the risk of operating if they had known the shell was so close to her spine. If, during the operation, the bullet had touched the spine, she could have been in a vegetable state, sitting in a wheelchair for the rest of her life.

As Peggy sped off towards the hospital, Victor stayed behind to keep guard in case the gang returned. Finally, Mark had reached a house with enough cell phone reception to call the police for help. The cops finally arrived - three hours later. They came without guns, were very relaxed, and dressed like they were going out on a lovely and relaxing drive to the beach.

Life would drastically change after this dramatic event. For some time, it would be nothing like it used to be. Almost every day, for some weeks, the Ywamers had to deal with unannounced reporters visiting the base. Oscar and Nathalie were quieter at school since the news of the shooting was announced nationwide. Oscar had usually sat at his desk in his room to do homework and to study for O-levels. Now he sat on the front porch with his notebook, getting a good view of the whole campus and most of the tree line. Behind him, stacked in perfect order, was an assortment of machetes, axes, pick-axes, and hatchets. Trying to get him to concentrate fully on his homework would have been impossible. Instead, his eyes focused primarily on the thick jungle, where the masked cowards had disappeared into – knowing that any second they could return, had they noticed the three hours the police took to arrive at the crime scene.

Victor also changed that day. Even though he had already been a vigilant person, highly conscious about his family's security and well-being, that day made him double and triple his vigilance into anxiety and worry. Even though he didn't realize it, under the surface, it started affecting his health. After some months, Peggy, Oscar, and Nathalie observed that Victor would begin to show involuntary shaking in his left arm under certain strenuous circumstances. This at first happened when he would answer questions at an airport or concentrate on talking in English, which was no easy task for him and required his full attention. However, he was oblivious to his subtle shaking.

Only his loved ones perceived it, but nobody knew the problem. Some simply thought that he was overly nervous at times. But the family's time in Trinidad and Tobago was coming to an end.

An Unexpected Harvest

23

Some weeks had passed since that bloody Sunday. The tension was in the air, and the collective sense of alert was quite evident in the Ywamers' sobriety. It had been an attack to simply steal a car, and even though it wasn't a new car, it would have had a colossal monetary cost in Trinidad. Or could there actually be another hidden motive behind the attack? Could these five criminals be part of the radical Islamic group quite notorious in Trinidad? Was the shooting birthed out of hate for Christian missionaries? Or did someone want to scare the foreigners into leaving the island, being free to take possession of the enormous land? Nobody really knew why the event had happened, thanks to the overly relaxed police force, which never really developed a serious investigation into the attack.

Kevin and Sue were busy still recovering from their wounds. Oscar and Nathalie couldn't focus on their studies very well, and having to walk through the jungle to reach the main road every morning to go to school was proving to be a challenge to the imagination, which would create mental movies of masked assailants jumping out of the bushes with their weapons once again. So for the first couple of nights after the attack, most of the women and children were sent to sleep in Mark's apartment, which was in the middle of a more urban setting, less isolated, and, therefore, safer.

Victor was more alert than ever, he didn't only just have his senses at maximum alert, but a new level of anxiety had taken home in his soul, which gradually took a quickening toll on his body. After approximately three months, Victor noted a subtle but continuous sensation of electricity that ran along his fingertips. At first, he thought it was some strange and novel manifestation of the Holy Spirit upon him. Then he started to be aware of the tremors, and upon diagnosis, he received the doctor's verdict.

"Don Victor, I'm so sorry to inform you... that you have Parkinson's disease." Parkinson's was a sickness that Victor learned would have a gradual and progressively stronger effect on his nervous system as time went by. Victor remembered the vision he had received some time ago.

Three weeks before the tremors caused by Parkinson's became evident, one morning, Victor and Peggy, along with the DTS students, were spending time together in prayer. In that meeting, Victor had a vision in which he saw himself in a room surrounded by friends and family, his wife, and children. He was his usual self, telling funny stories and jokes, causing the others to chuckle. The only two aspects of this picture that started to disturb him were the wheelchair upon which he sat... and the tremors that shook his fragile body.

That day a lie entered Victor's mind and heart; that God had sent him this sickness and wasn't going to heal him - for His glory. This lie started to take effect in his life, for Victor accepted the disease as part of himself, which became a burden for him in the years he had ahead. Every once in a while, Victor would run into prophets, men of God, pastors, and evangelists, and countless times these people, amongst many others, would pray for healing over him. Still, he didn't receive healing for some reason. Parkinson's naturally spread over his body, first to both arms, then it weakened his knees, and Victor had to start taking medicines on a daily basis in order to rest for some hours from the constant tension that he experienced.

The Lord decided to turn the situation of Parkinson's to his advantage. Victor continued to be invited to different cities in Colombia to teach in the DTS and SOSM (School of Strategic Missions) in Ywam. At the end of each week of teaching, they would have a forty-five-minute session organized by the school leaders specifically for the students to give feedback about what they learned and, in a certain way, to honor the invited speaker. They would usually comment on their favorite points of the week and what impacted their lives most. Victor had taught the topics of Spiritual Warfare and Hearing God's Voice for many years, and usually, the students would give remarks about his passion for the Lord, his heart of a father, or his obedience to the Lord; but now Victor started hearing a new line.

"Teacher, what most impacted my life in this week's teachings was the fact that despite the Parkinson's, you talk about Jesus with so much passion, and you are obedient to the Lord in making these long trips when you could be comfortable at your home, with Parkinson's being a valid enough reason to not make the journey... You could simply retire, but you have still decided to invest in us. Thank you, Victor."

In 2006, after living in Trinidad and Tobago for about three years, Oscar was sixteen and set off to have his own experiences and adventures with the Lord in Puerto Rico. Nathalie, 12, was progressing in her studies despite the language barrier. She was an instrument of God that filled the family's home with smiles, joy, and uncontrollable episodes of laughter. In only a few years, she would set out on her own journey with Jesus in New Zealand.

The visa that the family members had for Trinidad were limited to three years, and to renew or extend them, they would have to leave the country for a year and, upon their return, pay a fee of a couple thousand dollars. This one-year gap would be a massive interruption in Nathalie's studies. Victor and Peggy had reached their goal of pioneering the DTS and training a local Trinidadian through mentorship who would continue running the schools.

So they began the return journey to Colombia. Even though they had many farewells organized for them during those last weeks in Trinidad, there was a sense of relief amongst the family. Trinidad had been a harsh and, at times, cruel host. There were many war wounds in need of healing, both emotional and physical. On many occasions, Victor and Peggy could have given up under their significant burdens and aggravating circumstances. Still, they persevered to the end of their time there.

"Good and faithful servant..." were the words that resounded in Victor's heart as he left Trinidad. Victor and his family had faced the jungle, slept with spiders, housed both invited and uninvited snakes in their home, swam with caimans, survived a five-man armed assault, put up with the local racism, and taken many young people to Nigeria, Tanzania, United States, and India to live their first adventures with the Lord.

In Colombia in 2007, Victor and Peggy felt the Lord's guidance to return and settle in Bucaramanga, Colombia. They established themselves in their old house in the Los Naranjos neighborhood. They reconnected with the Ywam base and soon enough were helping teach in the DTSs and reconnecting with local churches they had known before they left for Trinidad. As they heard about what had been happening amongst churches and Ywam bases, Victor and Peggy received an enormous surprise. Prayer groups had been established in some churches in

Bucaramanga. Their prayer focus: China and Tibet. These were churches in which Victor and Peggy had invested much time and energy, and now they were giving fruit for the salvation of the nations.

In Ywam Cartagena, a group of young people from different cities had come together with a sole purpose: to embark on a journey to China and establish themselves there, some amongst the Chinese and some amongst the Tibetans. Most of the groups of King's Kids would soon be leaving on outreaches to China. Other Ywamers, who weren't leaving immediately, had made strong commitments to go to Asia and to pray for her nations. Entire families would move to the Eastern Giant with the goal of transforming the Land of Mao into the Land of Jesus Christ. Hearing those reports brought tears to the veteran missionary's eyes. He had invested six years in Colombia, challenging youngsters and equipping churches to go out and bless China without seeing a single good fruit. Now, hundreds were praying and interceding for China, and dozens were preparing and equipping themselves to walk the road towards the Eastern Giant. China was now at the heart of Ywam Colombia; it was on their map of destinations.

God's calling to Oscar had also been confirmed during his time in Puerto Rico: he would also go to sow his life in Asia for many years. Nathalie, a brave and courageous young lady, would go on to become quite the artist, a fantastic mother and wife, investing much of her life in the youth in Switzerland. And Peggy, that priceless treasure, the greatest blessing to Victor the warrior, was at his side as leader of the base of Bucaramanga.

Victor sat on the balcony of the countryside house the Lord had provided for them, overlooking Bucaramanga in the distance. His heart was glad as he meditated on and remembered all the goodness that his Father had bestowed upon him. From his small beginnings in the neighborhoods in Bogota to the multiple trips around the world, his family, and all those special people with whom he had had the privilege of working; for whom he had been incredibly blessed. He couldn't ask for anything more. Tibet and China were deeply anchored in his memories, even though they now shared houses with England, Russia, India, Tanzania, and of course, Colombia.

The Lord had decided to turn the situation of Parkinson's to his advantage. Victor continues to be invited to different cities in Colombia to teach in the DTS and SOSM (School of Strategic Missions) in Ywam. At the end of each week of teaching, they have a forty-five-minute session organized by the school leaders specifically for the students to give feedback about what they learned and, in a certain way, to honor the invited speaker. They would usually comment on their favorite points of the week and what impacted their lives most. Victor had taught the topics of Spiritual Warfare and Hearing God's Voice for many years, and usually, the students would give remarks about his passion for the Lord, his heart of a father, or his obedience to the Lord; but now Victor started hearing a new line.

"Teacher, what most impacted my life in this week's teachings was the fact that despite the Parkinson's, you teach with so much passion, and you are obedient to the Lord in making these long trips when you could be comfortable at your home, with Parkinson's being a valid enough reason to not make the journey... You could simply retire, but you have still decided to invest in us. Thank you, Victor."

Victor – and his whole family – had seen the power and love of God in many tangible and undisputed manners, which were carved onto their hearts. If he was passionate for Jesus when he started his walk with the Lord many years ago, he was twice as passionate and intimate with the Lord now. He hoped and looked forward to the day he would finally see his heavenly Father, Boss, and Best Friend, face to face, forever.

Yes, Victor still struggles with Parkinson's and has been doing so since 2005. But just like Job, Victor never blamed the Lord for his illness – as you will see ahead. On one occasion, a believer approached Victor after some sort of prayer meeting and said to him,

"Brother Victor, it's so sad to see you this way. I don't understand. Why would God send you this illness? You have served the Lord all your life as a missionary in many countries, and you've sacrificed so much for Him. I don't get it!"

"Dear brother, the Lord didn't send me this illness. He is a good Father. What kind of father would send their child a disease like this? Parkinson's is a result of my anxieties, my excessive worry, and maybe due to my lifestyle before I became a Christian."

Victor never complained about his illness. Yes, it affected him, and during his teaching sessions, sometimes he would suddenly feel completely lost and disoriented, forgetting what he was talking about at times. But as he remained obedient to the Lord and then with humility continued to speak after admitting his weakness, he impacted the lives and hearts of those who watched him. And well, even though the disease was getting worse, the doors started to open little by little for the possibility of having brain surgery, which would cure him of most of the symptoms and effects that Parkinson's brought upon Victor's nervous system.

Victor – sixty-two years old – sat and rested on his balcony. A thought crossed his mind,

"Lord, I've had a good life, and I thank you for it every day. You gave me some precious children and the best wife in the entire universe. But, if my time is drawing to an end, I would be happy to go and rest in your arms."

But the answer he received from the Lord was a gentle and kind rebuttal to his request.

"I'm not done with you yet, Victor. You still have many kilometers to walk ahead of you on this earth, with me."

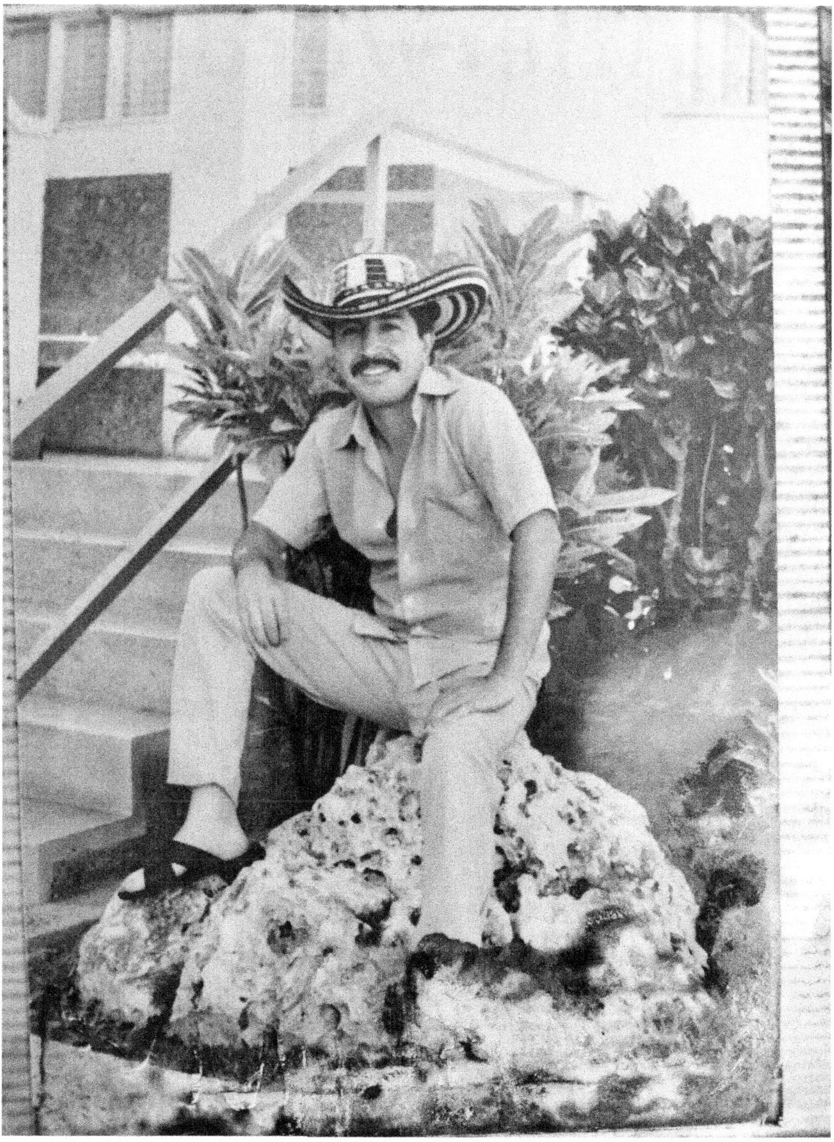

Afterword

Victor sat in the living room of "The Pearl" - not the ship from a Pirates movie, but the name they gave to their family home, located in the mountains surrounding Bucaramanga. There was a visitor for the weekend - it was and continues to be common to have people visit Victor and Peggy for a time to receive some rest, prayer, and counseling. In these visits, without exception, there would be times when Victor would tell a story, or two, or ten... anyway, they were all from his past experiences. They ended up being able to guide the visitor or couple in question to see God more authentically or intimately in their own lives.

Many Christians in Colombia struggle with the idea of actually going out as missionaries, and that can be due to many reasons. Some still think that all countries in South America are still only a mission field and cannot be a missionary-sending force. Many also believe that missions are only possible for "Gringos" because we don't have enough money for those long and expensive travels. It's hard for them to believe that the Lord will provide for them if they took steps of faith to obey Him in taking the Gospel of Jesus to the ends of the earth. Victor came up against these giants before he went to China, and many thought he was crazy for it. But the Lord's provision for His children is global; His faithfulness is not limited to people hailing from one or two wealthy countries.

It is my hope that Colombians, South Americans, and any number of others that may pick up this book will understand that Jesus' criteria for sending his disciples and commissioning them to go to the ends of the earth with the Gospel weren't an impressive bank statement, a well-covered budget for their projected duration as disciples, or even the backing of a wealthy congregation or family, or a certain level of education and experience. Instead, the requirement was simply love, the love that Jesus talks about, which implies obedience to his commands.

If He could trust in and change the world with those simple fishermen, those tax collectors (who weren't exactly the most spiritual people on earth at that time), and if he could take a simple Colombian coming from a broken life, a broken family, on the brink of suicide, and transform him into a man who became the first Colombian missionary in taking the Gospel to China and Tibet, and who thanks to now, many of his disciples are in the uttermost parts of the earth sharing the love of Jesus, and walking every day by faith, making more disciples as they go. He can definitely change the world through you. Your background doesn't matter, your financial ability doesn't matter, your family, your church, your eloquence, your intelligence, none of it defines whether or not Jesus can choose you to walk, taken by His hand, set on making history. All you have to do is say yes to Him and seek Him with all your heart.

    I genuinely hope you have been blessed while reading this book, as much as I have been blessed by sitting down with this hero, who has been my best friend, and listening to his life stories, writing this book. May the Lord draw closer to you, and may you draw closer to Him. May His face shine upon you, and may many come to know Him by seeing Him shine through you.

    As a good friend of mine always says: "The best is yet to come."

Acknowledgements

This work's writing, development, and completion wouldn't have been possible without the help, advice, support, and encouragement of exceptional people whom I highly admire and regard. Many more friends and family should be mentioned here but aren't because it would take a whole other book!

Ricardo I. Rodriguez and Marilú Ayala have been family friends to Victor and Peggy for over thirty years.

Rosa Rocha and John Fries have been such an encouragement in the process of writing this book. Their hospitality is renowned. It has been a true blessing to have their support and love.

Nick and Paula Watts, whom I met in India at the foothills of the Himalayas, and later on had the privilege of staying with them as their first guest in San Diego, for their support and willingness to help in the editing process.

Heather Findley, who gave her skills in English to do all the final touches to the script to make it readable.

My dear friend Stephanie Pinilla who put so much effort, skill, and dedication into the superb front and back cover design. Her skill, friendship, and support were a constant.

To my family, my dear parents and sister, for being the greatest support I could ever have imagined on this earth. They've really been a flesh-and-bone picture of humility, love, and unbreakable faith. I can confidently say I'm the luckiest son and brother to be walking this earth. I wouldn't be serving the Lord if it weren't for their prayer and intercession.

And Jesus, the Holy Spirit, and the Father are due the highest acknowledgment here. Victor wouldn't have had the life change you read about without them. Without them, there would be no missions, no Gospel, no life, no hope, no inspiration, nothing – period. The Lord's friendship and grace towards me have been my greatest support. He is the center of every chapter in this book; without Him, there would be no story. Every miracle was thanks to Him; every inspired line came from Him. Only He can change lives, and He wants to change them through you.

Erik J. Churchill

Printed in Great Britain
by Amazon